How to Raise Capital from Middle Eastern Investors

Cultural awareness training is sometimes perceived as a luxury within the business world.

LESSON ONE:
Middle Eastern write from Right to Left.

AARON DABBAGHZADEH

InwestCo
Investor Club

How to raise capital from Middle Eastern investors
Cultural awareness training is sometimes perceived as a luxury within the business world.

Copyright © 2022 Aaron Dabbaghzadeh
All Rights Reserved.

ISBN: 978-0-578-38121-3

All rights reserved. No part of this book may be reproduced or transmitted in any form or by any means, electronic, or mechanical, including photocopying or recording, or by any information storage and retrieval system without permission in writing from the author.

All translations of this work must be approved in writing by the author. Please contact INWESTCO LLC for permission to translate and distributions agreements.

Printed in the United States of America

To order more copies for your team, go to inwestco.com or contact INWESTCO LLC at +1 (424) 431-4042.

About the Author

Aaron Dabbaghzadeh is the CEO and Founder of InwestCo, an exclusive investor club that pairs entrepreneurs with the right investors to make long-lasting relationships.

Aaron is a seasoned entrepreneur with many years of expertise in Global Banking, Manufacturing, Investment Diversification, and Risk Management.

Coming from a Family Office with roots that date back 80 years in Real Estate, Agricultural, and Manufacturing in the Middle East and Europe, Aaron maintains Investor connections around the globe. His work in the ultra-wealthy investor arena has culminated in the establishment of an elite Private Investor Club over the course of the last 17 years. His global network of 1,900 registered investors has over $750 Billion Assets Under Management. His Club is comprised of private investors, venture capital firms, high-net-worth individuals, entrepreneurial ventures, investment fund managers, and other types of high-ranking professionals.

Aaron's extensive expertise in the United States, Europe, and the Middle East has positioned him as a well-rounded player in domestic and international markets. He has insight into what Investors are looking to invest in, where they feel most eager to invest their capital, and which platforms.

Prior to founding InwestCo, he held numerous top leadership positions, including Co-CEO of Mahtab Holding, operating in the Middle East, and Vice President of Global Risk Management at East West Bank in the United States and Greater China.

Mr. Dabbaghzadeh is actively involved in the day-to-day operations of InwestCo while overseeing the Company's business strategy, financial performance, and growth across all markets.

Aaron earned a Master of Business Administration from the University of California, Irvine, and a Master of Science in Engineering from IAU's School of Industrial Engineering.

Acknowledgments

The world is a better place as a result of individuals eager to innovate and lead. What makes it even better are people who volunteer their time to mentor aspiring leaders. Writing this book proved to be more challenging than I anticipated, and the journey was more rewarding than I could have imagined. However, none of this would have been possible without God's grace and the blessing and support of my friends and family.

To begin, I'd like to offer my heartfelt appreciation to my great friend and mentor, Dr. Virginia Alberts, for providing invaluable guidance throughout the book's creation. Working under her direction was a tremendous privilege and honor. I'd also like to express my gratitude to her for her friendship, sensitivity, unwavering support, and wonderful sense of humor.

Additionally, I am indebted to my parents, Azar and Mohammad, and the rest of my family for their love, prayers, support, compassion, and sacrifices in educating and preparing me for my future. I'm at a loss for words to express how much I love you and will never be able to repay you for everything you've done for me, but I can say that I owe my life to you.

Special thanks to my great friends Amjad and Dara for always believing in me, supporting me through all of my ups and downs, and assisting me in becoming the best version of myself, as well as to everyone at the InwestCo for enabling me to be the CEO of a company that I'm honored to be a part of.

Finally, and most significantly, I want to express my sincere gratitude to the love of my life, EHH, for her unconditional love, understanding, brilliant ideas, inspiration, and support in completing this project. It would not have been possible without your help and encouragement.

Disclaimer

This book is intended for information purposes only and is not a solicitation or offer to buy or sell any financial instruments.

You should never act on any casual advice or strategies from a book without getting counsel from your attorney, business advisors, or compliance team. For that reason, if you get advice to try out a new structure, pitching strategy, marketing strategy, or tactic in this or any other publication, always be careful to seek professional support before acting on it. I would strongly recommend looking into 506c SEC registration, 506b, potential qualified exclusions for single investor deals or funds of certain types, and making a careful review of the fund versus broker-dealer/FINRA versus RIA options.

Under no circumstances, including but not limited to negligence, will we be held liable or responsible, directly or indirectly, for any damage or loss, whatsoever, arising out of, or in connection with, the use of the information contained herein, including without limitation, direct, indirect, consequential, unexpected, special, exemplary or other losses that may result, including but not limited to economic loss or any other type of loss or damage, or unexpected or adverse reactions to the information and/or suggestions contained herein.

Table of Contents

About the Author 2
Acknowledgments 4
Disclaimer 6
Table of Contents 7
Overview 10
Middle East 12
    Gulf Cooperation Council (GCC) 14
    Primary Industries 16
    Future Vision 18
    Saudi Arabia and UAE's Key Statistics 26
    GCC Currencies 28
Business Relationships 30
Common Traits in Arab Cultures 32
    Family 32
    Religion 32
    Hierarchy 33
    Collectivist 34
    Honor/Shame 34
    Networks 35
    Consensus 36
    Nationalism 36
Language 38
    Classical Arabic 39

- Modern Standard Arabic 39
- Arabic Chat Alphabet 39
- Arabic Numerals and Numbers 40
- Sample Arabic text (vocalized) 41
- Some commonly used terms in Arabic 41

Cultural Attributes 43
- Market Penetration 43
- Decisions can take a long time 45
- Body Language 48
- Eye Contact and Smiling 49
- Greeting 50
- Body Gestures 52
- Environmental Consideration 54
- Speak in Vague Terms, Metaphors, and Stories 55
- Communicate Face to Face 57
- Know Your Audience 58
- Difference Between Arabs and Muslims 60
- Luxurious and Lavish Lifestyle 63
- Generosity and Hospitality 67
- Hosting the Arabs 70
  - What not to do 71
- Dress Code 72
- Food and Beverage Restrictions 75
- Gifts 78
- Islamic Calendar (Hijri) 81

Women in business in the GCC countries 84

Negotiation 86
    The Process of Negotiation 88
    Negotiation Tactics 90
        PLANNING 90
        OPENING 96
        BARGAINING 97
        CLOSING 104
    Negotiation Summary 106
How to Pitch to Arab Investors 107
    Drafting your pitch deck 109
    Branding 113
    Content Localization 118
    Business Cards 122
    One Liner 123
    Best Pitching Practices 125
    Pitch Deck 129
    Quality of Your Material 130
    The Cover 133
    Pitch Deck Content 134
Conclusion 139

Overview

We have witnessed an exponential growth in the number of investments made by Middle Eastern investors both inside and beyond the GCC zone during the last two years (starting in mid-2020); in particular, the Arab investors have made significant investments in the United States and Europe.

But what motivates these initiatives?

In order to fully discourse this question, we should first recognize and understand the culture as it is very critical in many foreign countries.
It is worth noting that there are considerable cultural differences between the United States and the rest of the world. These differences range from scheduling business meetings, a formal greeting, or even a simple dress code which can make a major impact when dealing with international consumers, partners, and clients.
Lacking a solid understanding of the local culture influences the decision-making process and can result in the failure of any venture.

Therefore, before engaging in any business in the Middle East or meeting with a Middle Eastern investor, it is imperative to learn about business culture, business etiquette, meeting protocols, and negotiation techniques.

Through such knowledge, stereotypes are broken, and communication barriers are reduced.

This guide represents a comprehensive summation of tips on raising capital from Middle Eastern investors and doing business in the Middle East.

So, what are the first questions that come to mind when someone speaks about the Middle East?

- Where is the Middle East?
- Who are Arabs?
- Why are they so wealthy?
- What is their lifestyle?
- How are they growing so fast?
- How do they do business?
- With whom are they currently doing business?

Middle East

The Middle East is a semi-arid region in Southwest Asia and part of North Africa that extends from the Persian Gulf to the Mediterranean Sea. It is flanked on the north by the Caspian and Black Seas, on the south by the Sahara Desert and the Indian Ocean. Initially, the term "Middle East" was used to refer to the region east of the Balkans and the Ottoman Empire (Near East), and west of India.

While the phrase has gained popularity, it is still relatively new. It was coined by the British Foreign Service at the turn of the nineteenth century and was first used in 1902 in an article by a United States Navy commander.

It has a long-shared history and religious tradition as the three major monotheistic religions, Islam, Christianity, and Judaism, originated there. Additionally, it is frequently regarded as a center of commerce and cultural transmission.

There is often debate over the precise list of countries considered to be part of the Middle East region, however most people would agree that the following countries are included:

- Bahrain
- Egypt
- Iran
- Iraq
- Israel
- Jordan
- Kuwait
- Lebanon
- Oman
- The Palestinian Territories
- Qatar
- Saudi Arabia
- Syria
- United Arab Emirates
- Yemen

Arabic, Persian (Farsi), Turkish, and Hebrew were the Middle East's four most widely spoken languages.

Saudi Arabia, Oman, Kuwait, the United Arab Emirates, Bahrain, Qatar, and Iraq are positioned on the eastern edge of a massive geological plate known as the Arabian plate, which is slanted downward from west to east. These countries are collectively referred to as the Arab world, and they are bound together not just by shared history, language, and religion; but, also, by the opportunities created by the abundance of energy resources, such as oil and gas, and other mineral reserves located there.

Gulf Cooperation Council (GCC)

The Gulf Cooperation Council (مجلس التعاون لدول الخليج), abbreviated GCC, is a six-country Middle Eastern political, military, and economic alliance comprised of Saudi Arabia, Kuwait, the United Arab Emirates, Qatar, Bahrain, and Oman. The GCC was founded in May 1981 in Riyadh, Saudi Arabia.

The GCC's mission is to unite its members around shared objectives and common political and cultural identities that are deeply founded in Arab and Islamic cultures.

The GCC's principal decision-making entity is the Supreme Council, which meets annually and is composed of GCC heads of state. The Council's presidency is rotated annually.

From Left to Right: Sheikh Meshal al-Jaber al-Ahmad al-Sabah [Kuwait's Crown Prince], Sheikh Tamim bin Hamad Al-Thani [Qatar's Emir], Fahd bin Mahmud Al-Said [Oman's Deputy Prime Minister], Mohammed bin Salman [The crown prince of Saudi Arabia], Hamad bin Isa Al-Khalifa [Bahrain's King], and Sheikh Mohammed bin Rashid Al-Maktoum [The UAE's Vice President and Prime Minister] posing for a family photo during the GCC summit in Riyadh on December 14, 2021.

Primary Industries

So, why is it that the first thing that comes to mind whenever the Middle Eastern countries are mentioned is oil and gas?

The Answer is simple. The GCC countries' primary industries are oil and gas. After all, oil and gas are responsible for the transformation into the economic powerhouse the GCC is today.

Paleogeography explains why the Middle East has the world's largest oil reserves; almost a third of the world's oil comes from the Middle East today. Although the Middle East is currently renowned for its enormous deserts and plains; interestingly, this was not always the case. According to a widely acknowledged theory, over a hundred million years ago, the Arabian Peninsula of today was home to the Tethys Ocean which fed multiple rivers and was rich in nutrients and microorganisms.
Over time, the earth's tectonic movement resulted in the water drying up and layers forming on top of the previous sea; the organic remains were compressed and are presently harvested as fossil fuel.

It is worth noting that Saudi Arabia, Iran, Iraq, the United Arab Emirates, Kuwait, and Qatar are among the world's largest exporters of fossil fuels. Together they established the intergovernmental Organization of Petroleum Exporting Countries (OPEC).

Iran, Iraq, Kuwait, Saudi Arabia, and Venezuela founded OPEC from September 10–14, 1960, and eventually included countries like Qatar, Indonesia, Libya, and the United Arab Emirates.

OPEC's mission is to integrate and coordinate Member Countries' petroleum policies in order to provide: stable and fair prices for producers; an economical, efficient and consistent supply of petroleum to consumers; and, a decent rate of return on investment for those engaging in the industry.

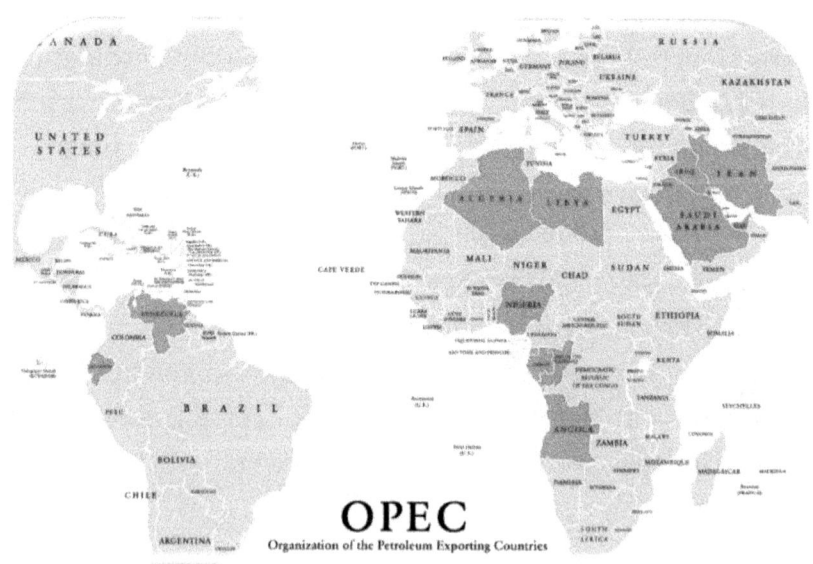

Future Vision

Due to the fact that the GCC countries are well aware of the finite nature of these nonrenewable resources, they have implemented measures to diversify their investments and revenue streams in order to pursue new opportunities and regulate emissions to combat global warming. As a result, the GCC countries are actively seeking new ways to diversify their economies away from crude oil earnings through the development of new industries and investment opportunities.

Subsequently, the aerospace and automotive industries are the pioneers.

Additionally, as tourism to the Emirates continues to rise, there are prospects for expansion in the hospitality, food, and beverage businesses.

Saudi Arabia's interest in hydrogen is an excellent example of diversification as well because it is motivated, primarily, by the need to assure economic security. Hydrogen can assist the world's largest crude oil exporter in meeting key Saudi Vision 2030 mandates which include diversifying exports, leveraging existing supply chains to improve local content, and establishing new industrial sectors.

Saudi Arabia has set a goal of being the world's largest supplier of hydrogen.

Hydrogen production would allow them to become less reliant on fossil fuel as the key source of income from international markets.

This may be of great value to the country in the carbon-constrained initiative that is characterized by the wave of net-zero targets from industries and governments worldwide.

Saudi Crown Prince Mohammed bin Salman's economic reform agenda envisions the Kingdom's capital becoming one of the world's largest cities (in the top ten). The Kingdom is investing billions of dollars to make Riyadh a global city by 2030. According to the capital's royal commission president, it is expected to attract sizeable investment from foreign investors as well as the private sector.

Sharma's transformation is one of the new objectives of Saudi Vision 2030. Sharma is a desolate coastal village in Saudi Arabia's northwest corner, near the Gulf of Aqaba and Egypt's coastlines; it has limitless access to seawater but only a few dozen residents. Nonetheless, the Crown Prince has a vision for this city to become a $500 billion city-state, spanning 10,000 square miles of rocky desert, named NEOM.

The September 2018 documents provide limited insight into NEOM's strategy and roadmap, considering the initiative was only introduced in 2017.
NEOM is positioned to be a futuristic tech center that will outperform Silicon Valley in technology, Hollywood in entertainment, and the French Riviera in tourism.
It is expected to attract the world's brightest brains and talents; officials anticipate the first arrivals in 2024.

According to the project's CEO, Nadhim Al-Nasr, they initially encountered difficulties as they attempted to create a city around technology that did not yet exist; but, they are undoubtedly on the right track.

According to Joseph Bradley, CEO of NEOM Tech and Digital Company, the project is on the cutting edge of cognitive solutions and artificial intelligence and is exploring novel approaches to resolving the "data privacy problem."

NEOM's next step is to get approval for the special regulations that will establish it as a "free zone" with laws distinct from the rest of Saudi Arabia.

Designs for the new city-state include Neom Mountain, Image Source: Wall Street Journal

On a similar note, H. H. Sheikh Mohammed bin Rashid Al Maktoum, Vice President and Prime Minister of the UAE and Ruler of Dubai, announced the UAE's comprehensive roadmap and future strategy for the country's development.

Dubai is seen as the cosmopolitan embodiment of the new Arab ambition and wealth. It is viewed as the GCC countries' sandbox for testing and assessing the feasibility of new ideas and projects prior to implementing them across the region.

Dubai is renowned for its avant-garde architecture, upscale shopping, and vibrant nightlife. Within a short period of time, the city was converted into a sandcastle in the public's eyes, astounding everyone in the region and beyond.

Some western business mind executives are still hesitant to expand their reach into these unknown regions; as to their knowledge, these lands are still somewhat of a mystery to the world and are stuck in the twenty-first century.

It is essential to know that Dubai is one of the United Arab Emirates' seven emirates and the fact that Abu Dhabi is the United Arab Emirates' most prominent powerhouse.

During the glory days of 2002-2007, Dubai captured the heart and imagination of investors. However, it was Abu Dhabi, Dubai's wealthier, more conservative elder brother, who came to Dubai's rescue during the financial crisis.

Despite the fact that the oil industry was once the backbone of Dubai's economy, oil and natural gas now account for less than 6% of revenues; this reflects a successful diversification away from an oil-based economy. The UAE's enormous hydrocarbon wealth gives it one of the world's highest GDP per capita, where its brother Abu Dhabi owns the majority of these resources -95% of the oil and 92% of the gas. Thus, Abu Dhabi controls 9% of the world's proven oil reserves and about 5% of the world's natural gas reserves. Noteworthy, here, is the fact that Dubai's oil reserves have dwindled dramatically; and, they are anticipated to be depleted within the next two decades.

H. H. Sheikh Khalifa bin Zayed Al Nahyan, President of the UAE, initiated a long-term strategy to revamp one of the world's top oil exporters' economies. This new strategy will propel the country forward by identifying future challenges and requirements, solving them through impactful long-term programs, and capitalizing on new global development opportunities.
The strategy is centered on three main themes:

- Constructing national capacity
- Setting strategic priorities for the future
- Establishing a new operational model for the government

Future prototypes for various sectors, including education, social development, healthcare, and the environment, are being designed as part of the new plan. These will lay the groundwork for future government policymaking.
The new approach includes developing national human competencies in all major industries, improving international relationships, and establishing specialized research and development labs to analyze future challenges and opportunities.

Planning will become a required component of government departments' operations under the new strategy. Future scenario reports on critical sectors will be released and evaluated to assist governments in creating strategies and policies.

Recent regulatory reforms have made the country more business-friendly and enabled investors to apply for long-term visas.

- One of the most exciting changes in these reforms is the suspension of the necessity of having a local managing partner to operate a business. Foreigners will no longer be required to have an Emirati shareholder or agent when establishing a company in the United Arab Emirates, which is a positive modification to UAE company legislation. (However, some industries considered to be strategically important are exempt from the new laws; these sectors include energy and hydrocarbons, telecommunications, and transportation.)
"The modified Commercial Companies Law intends to strengthen the UAE's competitive edge and is part of the UAE government's efforts to make conducting business easier," Economy Minister Abdulla bin Touq Al-Marri was quoted as saying.
The UAE proposed a law permitting 100 percent foreign ownership of enterprises from 1 June 2021; the move is one of the numerous measures aimed at attracting investment and foreigners to the Gulf state which has been significantly impacted by the coronavirus outbreak. Additionally, the Commercial Companies Law has been revised multiple times to include adjustments to corporate governance and capital

raising provisions as well as meeting procedures. These regulations took effect on 2 January 2021 and required onshore businesses to amend their Articles of Organization by 2 January 2022 to ensure compliance with the newly updated provisions.

- The United Arab Emirates established a new system for long-term residency visas in 2019, making it much easier for foreigners to live, work, and study in the UAE.
  The Golden Visa system is designed to grant long-term residency (5 to 10 years) to individuals with exceptional talents such as: medical experts; researchers; those in scientific industries and specialized academics; and investors. The Golden Visa will provide extra security for expatriates, investors, or anybody wishing to relocate to the UAE. Most applicants must have at least 10 million AED in public investment, either in the form of a fund or a firm.

  However, some restrictions apply.
  For example:

     o At least 60% of the overall investment must be liquid; not in real estate.
     o The invested capital must not be borrowed.
     o In the case of assets, the investor must own the entire asset.
     o The investor must hold the investment for a minimum of three years.

This 10-year visa could be extended to include business partners with a minimum contribution of 10 million AED from each partner. Additionally, the visa holder's spouse and children as well as his firm's executive director and advisor may be included on his long-term visa.

- As part of the reform, the UAE implemented Saturday and Sunday weekends starting Jan. 1, 2022; this also applies to federal government enterprises. The adjustment is important, given that Friday has always been regarded as a holy day for Muslims. The majority of Gulf countries have weekends from Friday to Saturday. The UAE will operate on a 4.5-day week, with the weekend beginning on Friday afternoon and concluding on Sunday. The UAE workday is, normally, eight hours long, from 9 a.m. to 5 p.m.; however, during Ramadan, most only work six hours a day.

- Prior to recent developments, flexible work arrangements in the United Arab Emirates were few and far between; but, things have begun to improve in this area as well. Two new government resolutions that were introduced in 2019 encourage flexible employment arrangements. The resolution on part-time work is designed to aid businesses in meeting labor shortages, particularly during off-peak hours. Similarly, a remote working policy has been devised to aid Emirati employees in reaching a more balanced work-life ratio.

Saudi Arabia and UAE's Key Statistics

Countries	Saudi Arabia	UAE
Population	34,783,757	9,856,612
Median Age (years)	30.8	38.4
Population Growth (% per year)	1.62%	0.62%
Net Migration (per thousand, per year)	5.04	-3.18
Males / Females	1.05	1.06
Life Expectancy (years)	76.4	79.37
Arable Land (% of total land area)	1.5%	0.50%
Renewable Water (m^3 / person)	69	15.2
Population Density (people / km^2)	16.1	117.9
Real GDP[1] (Billions)	$ 1543.24	$ 655.79
GDP Growth Rate (% per year)	-0.9%	0.80%
GDP / Capita (USD / person) (@ PPP)	$ 44,300.00	$ 67,100.00
Private Consumption / GDP (%)	41.3%	34.90%
Government Consumption / GDP (%)	24.5%	12.3%
Investment Fixed Capital / GDP (%)	23.2%	23%
Investment Inventories / GDP (%)	4.7%	1.80%
Exports / GDP (%)	34.8%	100.4%
Imports / GDP (%)	28.6%	-72.40%
Unemployment Rate (%)	6%	1.60%
Gini Coefficient	45.9	32.5
Literacy Rate (%)	97.6%	97.6%
Government Surplus / GDP (%)	-8.9%	-0.2%
Public Debt / GDP (%)	17.2%	19.7%
Inflation Rate (% per Year)	-2%	-1.9%
Current Account / GDP (%)	1%	4%
Current Account / Capita (USD/Person)	$ 438.00	$ 2,685.00
EIU Democracy Index	2.08	2.9

---

[1] GDP = Consumption + Investment + Government Spending on Goods and Services + (Exports − Imports)

WWW.INWESTCO.COM

Private Saving[2] / GDP (%)	38%	46.8%
Electricity Production/Capita(kWh/Person*year)	9,317	12357
Net Oil Exports Per Person (bbl/person*year)	77	119
Carbon Dioxide Emission / Capita (tones/person*year)	16.2	20.9
Military Spend / GDP (%)	6%	5.6%

You can access the key statistics for other countries in the Middle East from the following links:

www.cia.gov/the-world-factbook/countries
www.eiu.com/

---

[2] Private Saving + Government Saving = Domestic Investments + Current Account

GCC Currencies

The following table details the currencies of the GCC members.

Country	ISO Code	Currency Name	Local Name
Saudi Arabia	SAR	Saudi Riyal	ريال سعودي
Kuwait	KWD	Kuwaiti Dinar	دينار كويتي
United Arab Emirates	AED	United Arab Emirates Dirham	درهم إماراتي
Qatar	QAR	Qatari Riyal	ريال قطري
Bahrain	BHD	Bahraini Dinar	دينار بحريني
Oman	OMR	Omani Riyal	ريال عماني

When we say the real exchange rate moves against a country's exporters (for example, the USA), we mean that the inflation rate of that country (USA); minus the inflation rate of its trading partner (for example, Saudi Arabia); has exceeded the rate at which the currency is depreciating; thereby putting the country's exporters in a disadvantageous competitive position.

$\%\Delta$ USD[3] inflation - $\%\Delta$ SAR[4] inflation > $\%\Delta$ USD[5]/SAR

---

[3] The United States Dollar; is the Currency of United States of America
[4] The Saudi Arabia Riyal; is the currency of Saudi Arabia
[5] USD is the Base currency (SAR/USD)

The aforementioned concept and appropriate hedging strategies will be discussed in greater detail in my forthcoming book, **"The Three Comma Club Strategies."**

So, now, that we have a fair understanding of the GCC countries growth strategies, it's time to dive deeper into their culture attributes and lifestyle.

Business Relationships

Business and personal friendships are the same because Arabs generally prefer to do business with people they know and like. Establishing friendships and relationships on the basis of personal trust ensures a strong bond. Small talk is more than just a courtesy; it is also a method to determine if you would be a suitable business partner. This is extremely effective since it not only provides you with access to shortcuts and local insights; but, it, also, provides you with someone who will be loyal to you, preserve your reputation, and come to your assistance if you should ever need it.

Being disconnected from the local population, in essence, disconnects you from the complex system of how things really get done. Most of the time, it is about who you know and how great of a friend you are, rather than what you know.

Since small talk is critical for developing good business relationships, you must be prepared to respond to questions regarding your travel, your home, your experience in the country to which you've traveled, your health, and the health of your family. Because of this, it is strongly recommended to engage in conversation freely and enthusiastically and to have several stories ready to tell, in order to break the ice, whenever the opportunity arises. And, it is, also, necessary for you to respond to your new acquaintance's questions.

Be aware that it is customary and expected to inquire about an Arab's family's health and some generic questions about their children; however, you must avoid specifically asking about female family members, as this may be considered offensive in more conservative societies.

Also, I suggest steering well clear of local politics, religion, or the royal family, unless (in the unlikely event) they seek your opinion on these matters.

Social networks are ingrained in the Middle East's business culture. As a result, you may discover numerous business prospects through the people you meet at social events. You never know who could be able to put you in touch with a decision-maker.

For instance, the UAE conducts a variety of networking activities and events. If you're new to the region, consider attending a few of these events to expand your business network. Similarly, you might contact the Dubai Chamber of Commerce, British Business Group, or Dubai Business Women's Council.

Common Traits in Arab Cultures

Family

The family or tribe takes precedence over all other considerations in everyday life. In such societies, people have extremely close bonds with a small group of people, whereas in more individualistic cultures, people form loose bonds with a large number of people. These family-centered societies frequently prioritize the family's interests. Therefore, nepotism is viewed as natural, and maintaining the family's honor is a top priority.

Religion

Arab culture and the Islamic faith are inextricably connected. Most Arabs believe that God controls and orchestrates most of life's events and that man is reliant on fate as determined by God and powerless to change their destiny. As a result, religious identification is essential to everyone in Arab society.

The majority of Arab officials believe that there should be no separation between mosque and state; and, that religion should be taught to children from a young age. Younger generations, on the other hand, are less conservative and have more support for the separation of religion and politics.

While Islam is the majority religion, other faiths are respected and treated with dignity.

Hierarchy

A hierarchical society is accustomed to authority levels. Management styles are an excellent example of how a hierarchical society varies from a more level society. In less hierarchical organizations, subordinates are expected to take the initiative, participate in decision-making, say "no" to their supervisor, and have an informal relationship with their superior. In a hierarchical society, the boss exercises complete control because that is his job. Staff will carry out specific commands and direction, meetings will be used to implement rather than discuss decisions, and all interactions with the boss will be formal.

Remember, unlike Western corporations, Arab organizations are not structurally visible to outsiders. So, work closely with experienced, respected local businesses or businesspeople to identify and reach the decision-makers who will be influential in your being able to close the deal.

Because the Gulf countries are hierarchical societies, their business culture is highly stratified, and the majority of businesses have a well-defined vertical structure. In most companies, older, more experienced employees get promoted to the top positions and are usually the primary decision-makers. On the other hand, lower-level employees often have less influence over decision-making, and they are prone to remain subordinate and follow orders from above.

Age, wealth, and family connections all contribute to an individual's status inside a corporation. The more of these an individual possesses, the more powerful they become. Additionally, there is a considerable preference for males over females, particularly at the higher levels.

Collectivist

This indicates that "we" takes precedence over "I" in such cultures. This collective mindset suggests that the group's interests, viewpoints, and decisions have a greater weight than the individuals.

Honor/Shame

In relationship-driven cultures, there is usually an emphasis on maintaining face, i.e., upholding the family/tribal honor. As a result, there are generally very complex engagement and communication style rules.

For example, in the Middle East, it is not customary to say "no" or openly disagree with individuals in order to save their faces. As a result, we see a lot of "beating around the bush" as people attempt to phrase sentiments in a way that avoids losing face. It is very common to say, "I will try," "Let's do our best," or "God willing" Instead of simply saying "no."

Praising someone improves their prestige, in addition to your standing as the praise giver. Paying for a restaurant's food bill is a simple yet effective way of gaining face and increasing your reputation for kindness.

On the contrary, face is lost or can be taken in instances where one has openly deviated from acceptable behavior. This could include being held accountable for something in front of others, failure to keep promises, or acting above or beyond your status.

Common ways foreigners tend to lose face in the region are in displaying impatience, anger, frustration, and complaining about local conditions, which are interpreted in the Middle East as simply showing a lack of manners.
That said, you should refrain from publicly correcting Arabs or bluntly criticizing someone's proposal in front of other attendees during a meeting or conference call. Take an indirect approach to all corrective remarks in order to avoid offending or embarrassing the other person.

Networks

Due to the reliance on connections and relationships in these cultures, networks are frequently used to accomplish tasks. Daily life is replete with intricate systems of favors and reciprocation, whether it's being introduced to the right people or getting around red tape. Associating with a network entitles you to resources.

Consensus

In hierarchical societies, decisions are frequently made collectively. Although the head of the family or tribe typically makes the final decision, in the Middle East, there is still a level of consultation with others known as "shura." Shura refers to the practice of polling the most knowledgeable individuals in order to come to the best choice. As a result, it is vital to develop relationships with company decision-makers and those who advise them to obtain the best outcomes.

Nationalism

Arab nationalism (القومية العربية) is an ideology that asserts the Arabs are a nation and advocates for their unity by glorifying the virtues of Arab civilization, the Arabic language and literature, and promoting the rejuvenation and political union of the Arab world.

Arab nationalists argue that the Arab nation existed as a historical entity prior to the rise of nationalism in the nineteenth century. The Arab nation developed gradually through time as Arabic became the dominant language and Islam advanced as a religion and civilization in the region.

Its core principle is that the Arab world's peoples, from the Atlantic to the Indian Oceans, constitute a unified country bound together by similar ethnicity, language, culture, history, identity, geography, and politics.

One of Arab nationalism's primary goals is to diminish the Western influence in the Arab world.

Traits in Arab Cultures

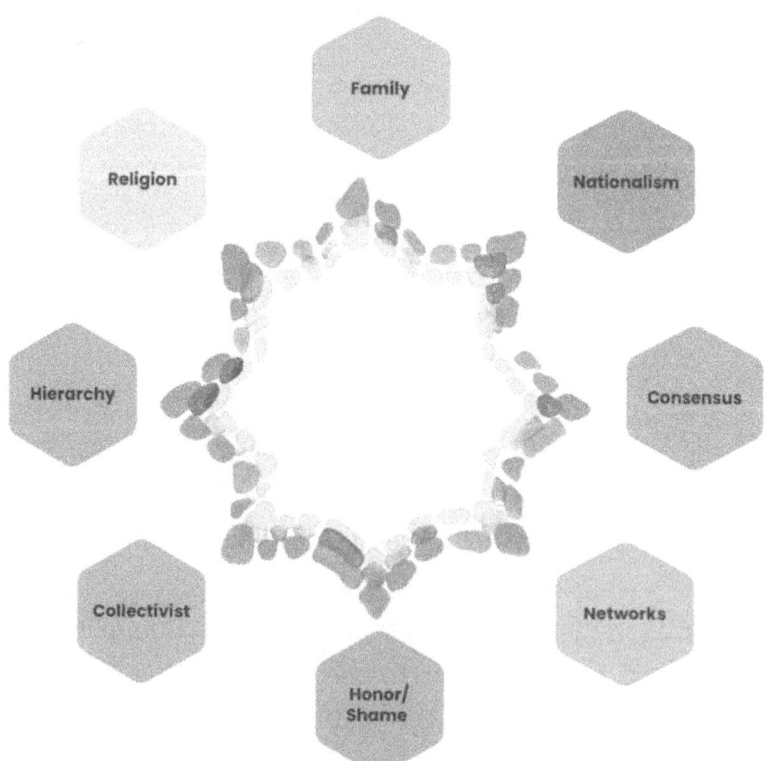

The al-Quds star (Arabic نجمة القدس) is a revered symbol in Islam and is frequently portrayed in Arab's artworks and architecture

Language

Gulf Arabs are extremely proud of their language and believe that it is incomparably different from any other language in the world. That is one of the reasons why they consider it to be a powerful unifying force in the Arab world.

The Islamic Caliphate era was a golden age for poets because they had the motive and pride to create their own poems and get heavily rewarded afterward by the caliph. As befitting a proud people, they put a lot of effort into keeping their classic language pure. Even after the Islamic conquests, when foreign influences moved in, scholars stealthily attempted to stem this tide.

Fasih Arabic (colloquial Arabic) is beautiful beyond description; and, the language ranks 6th among the world's major languages. Furthermore, Arabic is the language of prayer and worship for more than a billion Muslims around the world, as it is the language in which the Qur'an القرآن, the Holy Book of Islam, was revealed.

The Arabic alphabet consists of 28 letters, all of which represent consonants, and it is written from right to left. Like its contemporary Aramaic and Greek counterparts, the Arabic script is descended from the North Semitic alphabet. However, it was transformed to accommodate the more general phonology of the Arabic language and to a cursive style that was well suited for writing with a pen and paper.

Today there are two main types of Arabic:

Classical Arabic

The Qur'an and classical literature are both written in this language. It differs from Modern Standard Arabic mostly in terms of style and vocabulary, with some of the latter being archaic in nature. Even though all Muslims are obligated to recite the Qur'an in its original Arabic, many Muslims rely on translations in order to fully comprehend the book itself.

Modern Standard Arabic

The language that is universally understood throughout the Arabic-speaking world and can be spoken by almost all Arabic speakers. It is the language used in the great majority of written materials; and, informal television shows, lectures, and other presentations.

Arabic Chat Alphabet

If you're chatting online with an Arabic speaker who uses the Latin alphabet, you might come across the following letters:

ا	ب	ت	ث	ج	ح	خ	د	ذ	ر
a/e/è	b/p	t	s/th	j/dj/g	7	kh/7'/5	d	z/th/dh	r

ز	س	ش	ص	ض	ط	ظ	ع	غ	ف
z	s	sh/ch	s/9	d/dh/9'	t/6	z/th/dh/6'	3	gh/3'	f/v

ق	ك	ل	م	ن	ه	و	ي	ء
2/g/8/9/q	k/g	l	m	n	h/a/e/ ah/eh/é	w/o/ou/ oo/u	y/i/ee/ ei/ai/a/é	2

Arabic Numerals and Numbers

These numerals are those that are used for writing Arabic, and they are written from left to right. This type of numeral is referred to as "Indian numerals" (arqa-m hindiyyah) in the Arabic language. The word 'Arabic numerals' can also apply to the numbers 1, 2, 3, and so on.

٠	١	٢	٣	٤	٥	٦	٧	٨	٩	١٠
صفر	واحد	إثنان	ثلاثة	أربعة	خمسة	ستة	سبعة	ثمانية	تسعة	عشرة
ṣifr	wāḥid	iṯnān	ṯalāṯah	'arba'ah	ḥamsah	sittah	sab'ah	ṯamāniyyah	tis'ah	'ašarah
0	1	2	3	4	5	6	7	8	9	10

Sample Arabic text (vocalized)

يُولَدُ جَمِيعُ النَّاسِ أَحْرَاراً مُتَسَاوِينَ فِي الْكَرَامَةِ وَالْحُقُوقِ. وَقَدْ وُهِبُوا عَقْلاً وَ ضَمِيراً وَ عَلَيهِمْ أَنْ يُعَامِلَ بَعْضُهُمْ بَعْضاً بِرُوحِ اَلإِخَاءِ.

Some commonly used terms in Arabic

When/where to use	Transliteration	Arabic	English meaning
Initial greeting	As-salaam alaykum	السلام عليكم	Peace be upon you.
Response to above	Wa alaykum as-salaam	وعليكم السلام	And peace be upon you too.
Hello	Marhaba	مرحبا	
How are you?	Keif al-haal?	كيف الحال؟	
Response to above	Al-hamdulillah	الحمد لله	Thanks be to God.
Please	Min fadlak (to a male) Min fadlik (to a female)	من فضلك	

WWW.INWESTCO.COM

Thank you	Shukran	شكرا	
Expression common when discussing future plans or action	Insha'Allah	إن شاء الله	God willing.
This expression is usually said after giving a compliment, in the same way that you say be blessed or knock on wood	Masha'Allah	ما شاء الله	Another form of God willing
Mr.,	assayed	السيّد	
Ms.,	assayida	السيّدة	
Goodbye	Ma As-salama	مع السلامة	Go in peace.

In conclusion, learning a few words of Arabic is a simple approach to convey that a relationship is more than a business transaction, and eventually, your effort will be greatly appreciated.

Cultural Attributes

The following sections will explore Arab's cultural characteristics to familiarize you with their social conventions and behaviors.

Market Penetration

Gulf-based organizations are frequently multi-tiered and notoriously tough to penetrate.

As previously said, local business culture is centered on interpersonal interactions, consensus, and unit cohesion, whether familial, extended family, or company. Who you are and who you know (in Arabic: wasta) are critical in business circles. Wasta basically translates as "connections" or "influence," and its exact translation in Arabic is "middle."

Investing time in getting to know and trusting business acquaintances is time well spent. It is also beneficial to understand the particular interactions and influences between families (tribes) in Arab civilization.

It might take many formal and informal meetings to make tangible business progress. If a business partner requests a favor, make every effort to fulfill it or, at the very least, demonstrate that you made an attempt. Never refuse to perform something explicitly, even, when it is evident it is a waste of time.

Even if you cannot achieve what your contact needs or desires, your work, and passion will be remembered, appreciated, and most certainly compensated in due course.

Arab businesspeople are accustomed to inviting their partners to feast in order to develop a personal relationship. Accepting the invitation is a sign of good faith in the business relationship you are establishing.

Suppose you don't have an influential friend or business associate who can assist you in finding an entry point into a prospective customer's or investor's organization. In that case, you should think about engaging a professional intermediary with clout in order to save you money, time, and frustration in identifying and reaching the real decision-makers you want to target. Ideally, you might be able to call one of your existing suppliers/vendors or an individual with whom they have already done business in order to build a 'task force' to close the deal and prevent bottlenecks. When you are approaching a large deal, collaborating with experienced, local businesses or consultant firms makes a lot of sense.

Decisions can take a long time

Generally speaking, Arab cultures are risk-averse and hierarchical. Decisions are made from the top, often following discussions with other stakeholders of equal seniority. Once a decision is made, it is not questioned.

Furthermore, Arabs take time to gather additional information; hence, they choose indirect (high context) communication to convey implicit messages rather than direct communication (low context communication).

Arab society is categorized as a high-involvement culture; an Arab would like to ask as many questions as possible; yet the question must remain relevant to the negotiation's objectives.
They ask many questions because they want to plan carefully and gather as much information as possible to avoid a mistake before making a decision.

> To summarize, authoritative males make the final call on what to do, considering what serves the collective interest, while conferring and channeling from top to bottom, with consultations intensifying at the top and diminishing at the bottom.

Consultative authority is prevalent in Arab society, while discussions are typically informal and nonbinding. Nonetheless, in social organizational systems such as the family and tribe, the authority of those in charge faces constraints imposed by the collective consensus practices. As for business organizations, consultations seem to be superficial in the sense that the manager seeks to obtain the agreement of organizational members on decisions already made.

Still, this would be done in the context of projecting an image of true consultation and participation. Centralization of power and authority is evident in the context of a leader making decisions, after consultations, in the best interest of the collective. As such, the leader turns into an individual possessing dictatorial power and authority reinforced by followers' unquestioning loyalty and trust.

This mode of centralization is based on an essential managerial subscription to the assumptions of theory X in management. In other terms, followers or workers are lazy, do not want responsibility, are motivated by money, and must be tightly controlled using threats and punishment methods.

Consider how some Arabs may consider events as God destined. This is reflected in the frequently used phrase "Inshallah" (If God wills it). As a result, the success or failure of a deal is attributed, in part, to God's purpose. According to some American businessmen, this fatalistic mentality may contribute to his Middle Eastern colleagues' lack of urgency in business. There may be frequent references to God, the Prophet, and sacred texts throughout business dealings.

Patience is a precious virtue, and it gives others extra space and shows you are accommodating. Prepare to be adaptable and ready to handle altering schedules. Patience is the most valuable characteristic you can demonstrate throughout your professional and social life while living and working in the Gulf region. It is not uncommon for them to be late for appointments; however, it is critical that you do not adopt the same laid-back attitude.

Being impatient will have a negative impact on your character. Learn to display this most valuable quality even in the most frustrating business conditions, and you will, undoubtedly, reap the benefits.

Body Language

When it comes to the Arab world, body language is even more essential than the spoken word; and, it is equally as crucial as the spoken word since public disagreement is so dangerous. The way you move and communicate is continuously being monitored.

Your nonverbal communication and body language are being processed through the Arab value system just as if you were speaking. You should take note of any positive or negative body language reactions you notice and remember that this may be a more accurate indication of someone's thoughts than what they say out loud in conversation.

Familiarize yourself with the indications and extend hospitality in return; and, as a result, you'll get closer to the decision-makers and dealmakers.

Eye Contact and Smiling

Some Arab people prefer firm eye contact as a show of respect, while others would prefer that you politely avert your gaze when speaking to them.

But, you should avoid gazing at the opposite sex for more than three (3) seconds.

Just keep in mind that while dealing with Arabs, the "standard" for smiling is a little higher and your smile may not be met with the same level of enthusiasm.

Some Arabs believe that smiling too much can detract from your seriousness; so, they try to avoid doing, especially, while discussing a serious matter.

Greeting

In GCC countries, the standard first-contact greeting for men is a handshake, and when you first meet someone, you should address them as "Mr." or "Ms." Additionally, you should always begin with the eldest individual and work your way down in order of seniority.

When greeting a woman, wait for her to extend her hand before extending yours; you should avoid reaching out and simply maintain eye contact with her if she does not. It is customary in Arab culture to shake hands while greeting someone and before departing.

As a symbol of deference and respect, Arab men may embrace and/or kiss on the face, nose, or forehead. However, ex-pat guys are not expected to follow a similar manner. Kissing is strictly forbidden unless the other person draws you towards them and kisses you first. When welcoming someone, be cautious and offer to shake the other person's hand. Bear in mind that kissing among men is not, necessarily, a smack on the cheek; in some regions, you just kiss the air.

For the most part, men do this to other men, and women do this to other women. However, the most important question is how many times? Usually, three kisses are exchanged.

In Arab culture, it is completely acceptable for two guys to walk down the street hand-in-hand or to greet each other with a friendly hug when they first meet. This is something that children, teenagers, adults, and even hardened military personnel will do.

Arab manifestations of masculinity are simply non-restrictive when it comes to touching other males. All of this, of course, is irrelevant when discussing contact between members of the opposite sex. Bear in mind that same-sex touching is unaffected; it's, just, a show of friendship.

Finally, your new acquaintance may put their hand on their chest instead of shaking your hand as some conservative religious people don't like physical contact; especially, not with the opposite sex.

Body Gestures

Because of the widespread exportation of Western culture, the meaning of numerous body gestures that were formerly exclusive to specific contexts has become diluted. There will always be some who view things one way and others who perceive things another way, regardless of what different sources say. When it comes to body language, keep in mind that pointing and giving the thumbs-up signal are deemed disrespectful in Arab cultures, as is crossing your legs and exposing the sole of your shoe while seated.

Pay attention to how you're crossing your legs and feet in a meeting. Are your feet pointed toward somebody you're trying to impress, or worse yet, toward someone with higher status than you? They'd better not be!

Pointing is considered impolite, especially if you are face to face with someone.
Perhaps jabbing your finger in someone's face is considered rude in your local culture as well; in which case, you wouldn't do it in the first place. You may also witness Arabs turning their hands and raising their fingers upwards, towards the sky; this, typically, indicates that God decides destiny and they follow.

As you already know, checking your watch during a discussion sends a strong signal that you are bored and eager to leave. Interestingly, a similar motion is not uncommon during business meetings. Yes, in many Arab nations, checking your phone and sending a quick text message during a meeting is not, necessarily, impolite.

Those on the opposite side may be signaling with a raised eyebrow, reclining posture, or tone of voice that it's time to switch gears. Generally, you don't have to be concerned, as your instinct will guide you if you are on the lookout for non-verbal cues.

Environmental Consideration

A remark on personal space in the Arab world is essential at this point. Arabs frequently give you less personal space than Westerners; as a result, they will touch you more, stand or sit much closer to you, and may, even, grasp your hand when taking you somewhere. Although uncommon from a Western perspective, this behavior is simply a cultural difference. You should, however, be pleased if they do so, as it indicates that they feel close to you.

Meanwhile, always avoid stepping on anyone's toes; literally and symbolically!

Arabs traditional outfits usually require them to wear sandals. It's worth noting that many people in the Arab world find the bottom of the feet unclean. Therefore, they might require you to take off your shoes in some places, especially, sacred places such as mosques. The best practice is to keep an eye on the people around you and follow what they are doing.

Speak in Vague Terms, Metaphors, and Stories

Arabs frequently communicate in vague terms and in broad strokes during negotiations. For the Arabs, it is critical to get to know you personally before discussing business. They'll tell deceptive stories, employ metaphors, and sprinkle words with double meanings throughout.

This is not a deliberate attempt to irritate you but rather a style of communication that enables the exchange of ideas without jeopardizing the reputation of anybody else at the table.

Due to the fact that Arabs are not direct in their negotiations, you will need to understand how to circumvent and ask open, yet unobtrusive, questions in order to determine their mindset.

It's better if you're prepared to present a variety of options to see which ones seem to resonate the most with them.

Insulting prospective business partners with direct demands or rejections can spell the end of a relationship. Sustain a humble attitude and always pledge to evaluate requests. Similarly, you'll want to ensure that everyone in the room understands precisely what's on the table.

Arabs are unlikely to seek an explanation for fear of losing face; thus, it is up to you to ensure that all possible angles are covered. Nobody will sign a contract that they do not completely comprehend.

Avoid information overload with senior Arabs. Keep it brief and straightforward in bite-sized portions. Take extra care and effort to verify your message has been received correctly.

Nodding and smiling does not indicate agreement; they are indications of respect. Therefore, make it "short and simple" to avoid losing them in the details; and, allow time for comprehension.

A culturally sensitive Arab business negotiator can read the situation and pass on helpful signals.

Communicate Face to Face

Due to the importance of developing a personal relationship, it is critical that you meet face to face to establish mutual trust. For Arabs, it is essential to get to know you personally before discussing business. Compliments are expected at business meetings. Due to the importance of relationship-building in the culture, it is customary to compliment your counterpart and his organization.

Understand that you do not have a business opportunity if you are more than three feet from your Investor. Forget phone calls, emails, Facebook, and Twitter. Nothing replaces a personal visit.

If this is not possible, make a phone call. The written word is regarded as less personal and significant, and you may find that your letters and emails go unanswered for an extended period of time if you do not follow up by phone.

Certain countries, such as Saudi Arabia, do not conduct serious business with Western officials or even businesspeople over the phone; therefore, a personal visit is your only alternative.

Know Your Audience

While the GCC countries have a shared history and culture, they also have a great deal in common in terms of social attitude and corporate style.

Outsiders frequently make broad generalizations about Arab states and their people, which leads to the formation of stereotypes. However, inferences about Arabs are impossible because there is no such thing as a monolithic Arab society or culture. Each Arab nation's culture is unique and extremely rich; hence, there are distinctions both between and within countries.

Treating all Arabs similarly reeks of arrogance; and, coming across as arrogant is about the worst thing a western businessman can do in this region.

Furthermore, not all Arab women face oppression at the hands of their male counterparts. Women have a great deal of independence in several Arab countries. Similarly, not all women are obligated to wear veils. In Syria, Egypt, and Lebanon, women have the option of wearing a cover or not. Non-Muslims, however, are required to wear veils in some countries.

The traditional monarchy runs the government in Saudi Arabia, the United Arab Emirates, Kuwait, Bahrain, Qatar, and Oman. Yemen, Libya, Iraq, Syria, Tunisia, Lebanon, Egypt, and Algeria are constitutional republics. Lebanon's parliament is balanced between Druze, Christians, and Muslims.

Britain's Queen Elizabeth II and her husband, Prince Philip (L), stand with Abu Dhabi Crown Prince Sheikh Mohammed bin Zayed Al-Nahayan upon their arrival in the Emirati capital to tour the Sheikh Zayed Grand Mosque. (November 24, 2010)

Difference Between Arabs and Muslims

Muslim refers to a person who follows Islam as its religion and keeps faith in Allah. Remember, Muslim refers to religion while Arab refers to ethnicity.
Not all Muslims are Arab and not all Arabs are Muslim; however, the majority of the Arabs are Muslim.

Islam has diverged into two major branches: Sunnis and Shi'a.

Both Sunnis and Shi'a read the Quran, the Prophet's sayings, and both believe that Prophet Muhammad was Allah's messenger. Both branches adhere to Islam's five tenets:

- They fast during Ramadan,
- Swear to undertake a pilgrimage to Mecca,
- Engage in ritual prayer (which includes five daily prayers),
- Offer charity to the underprivileged,
- And pledge themselves to their faith.

Muslims pray five times daily with each prayer lasting approximately 15 minutes.

Prayer hours are communicated through the sounding of the call to prayer from local mosques (Adhan) and through the publication of daily news.

When setting up your meetings, you should be considerate and avoid these time frames as your Arab investors might be busy saying prayers. Even though they are allowed to say their prayer later in the day, the cultural norm and expectation are to say prayers on time and as a group.

The approximate timing of the five prayers are as follows; but, you can look up the exact timing on web:

1. Al-Fajr – Dawn, before sunrise
2. Al-Zuhr – Midday, after the sun has reached its highest point in the sky
3. Al-'Asr – Late afternoon
4. Al-Maghrib – Just after sunset
5. Al-'Isha – Between sunset and midnight

Ultimately, the fundamental ideological concerns about religious authority and leadership that arose after the Prophet's death divided Islam into two distinct branches.

- Sunni (followers of the Prophet's example - Sunnah) evolved to reference to those who followed the Prophet's closest companion (Abu Bakr).

- Those who adhered to the Prophet's cousin and son-in-law ('Ali) became known as Shi'a (the Party of Ali – Shi'atu Ali).

Sunnis adhere to the Prophet's example, whereas Shi'a follows Muhammad's family relatives through a succession of Imams, and they express their faith slightly differently.
Around 90% of Muslims worldwide are Sunni, whereas 10% are Shia. When in doubt, err on the side of caution and follow the locals' lead.

It is usually worthwhile to employ the services of an intermediary to assist you. Local chambers of business or a reputable local law firm can always help you. Additionally, the trade office of your home country's embassy will also be a competent port of call.

You usually find Arabs friendly and laid back but uncompromising about some topics; so, you have to be cautious as they might easily get offended.

In general, Middle Easterners are known to be slightly hot-tempered and stubborn; especially when it comes to their prophet, religion, politics, fundamental beliefs, and culture; however, that is not always the case.

Since western people are unfamiliar with Middle Easterners' communication norms and tone, they often think that they are arguing. Nevertheless, when you become more familiar with their cultural norms, you realize that they are typically loud and highly enthusiastic, especially when in a group. So, if you see a family yelling at each other in a public restaurant, they might, just, be very excited to see each other or may be insisting on paying the bill.

Luxurious and Lavish Lifestyle

Arabs are one of the most lavish people in the world; the simple life just doesn't suit them. In terms of living, eating, traveling, or most everything else, they just can't do or have something we refer to as "simple".

Throughout history, Middle Easterners in general, and Arabs in particular, have possessed an attitude of extravagance and luxury.

If you explore Arab architecture from the Middle Ages, you will see an excess of grandeur in the way structures were built and decorated. The palaces of the Arab Caliphs featured mercury-filled ponds where tiger-skin pillows floated for the purpose of relaxation.

Arab ladies wore pure gold belts encrusted with the rarest stones and clothing crafted from the finest silk, and sewn with gold threads imported from India and China.

Thousands of books were written and sleeved in gazelle skin; horses and camels were even adorned with silver and gold chains.

All of this occurred during Europe's darkest times. Even if you make a basic calculation and compare the combined wealth of the 50 wealthiest Arabs to the wealth of the 100 wealthiest persons in India, Arabs will still win. It's a $266 billion against $250 billion race. For Arabs, luxury is grandeur and opulence. Their vacations and style of living over a period of a week far exceed the average person's life savings; and, London is their most popular vacation destination.

However, this comes at a high cost. Arabs bring their expensive cars and stay in either their own private residences or the best suites money can lease. In fact, every summer, people in Los Angeles and London anticipate Arab car invasions which serve as eye candy for everyone else on the streets.

Given that religion shapes lifestyle, attitude, behavior, and social relationships in the Middle East, particularly in the Arab World, it should come as no surprise that people compete to show off God's gifts; a competition that manifests itself in fashion, food, cars, houses, lifestyle, and so on.

Arabs believe that wealthy people who do not exhibit their wealth have something to hide; and, such individuals would become the subject of gossip in Arab societies. You can't be wealthy and wear a Casio watch or drive a Ford Fiesta because people will assume you're afraid of something.

The same mindset has fomented a rally for good luxury manufacturers like LVMH and Swiss watchmakers to go above and beyond to access Middle East markets.

During the forecast period [2020-2025], the Middle East luxury goods market is expected to grow at a CAGR (Compound Annual Growth Rate) of nearly 8.5%.

In the Middle East, particularly in the GCC countries, 70% of consumers claim to have increased luxury goods spending. In recent years, the Middle East luxury goods sector has experienced rapid growth; and, has resulted in major companies expanding their brand distribution network and opening new stores in the region.

The region's growing economy and the population's high spending power have led to many new initiatives and brand opportunities. To build a leading platform for luxury products, particularly leather goods, in the Middle East, Chalhoub Group teamed with Farfetch in 2018.

Luxury goods are preferred over conventional goods by consumers in countries such as Saudi Arabia owing to their high purchasing power and long-term demand for these products that reflect their social status. Such factors have prompted companies to open serval boutiques in Saudi Arabia in order to capitalize on the market's potential.

Generosity and Hospitality

When it comes to generosity and hospitality, Arabs are renowned as masters of the art. Historically, this tendency stems from townspeople's willingness to host and feed desert visitors.

Arab hospitality's ultimate purpose is to honor a guest and break the ice; thus, relieving individuals of the "awkwardness" and fear associated with meeting a stranger.

Hospitality is a tradition in the Middle East. Generally, rituals are reserved for the most sacred of practices; in Arab culture, the way you treat your guest(s) falls under this sacred category. Hosts adhere to a strict routine for welcoming guests to ensure that all guests experience the same level of generosity regardless of the time of day or the time of year.

Due to the high value placed on hospitality, guests are welcomed into the family circle, even if they are strangers. The key to greeting a guest successfully is to create an ambiance of inclusion. By becoming a temporary part of the household upon arrival, the guest is protected from harm.

Ultimately, a true Arab will do all possible to make guests feel at ease, which also means that "no" is not an adequate answer.

In terms of the hospitality process itself, guests should be greeted outside the residence and escorted inside. They are, then, led to the best sitting area, where they will be inundated with an array of refreshments and treats.

Bear in mind that no amount of resistance will enable you to refuse food from an Arab host (believe me, I've tried). Regardless of how full you are, food will continue to flow until it is consumed. Why? Most hosts, sometimes, even, think their guests are either unable or hesitant to get another serving of food. So..., they continue providing and serving until the party ends; at which point, they offer their guests more food and treats to take with them.

You should take advantage of this exceptional treatment and accept it as customary so that the host can feel fulfilled in his obligation to pamper you in ways you never imagined possible.

Arab generosity is well-known; the majority of people are aware of the novelty that if you compliment whatever an Arab owns, they will insist on your taking it. This does occur, sometimes; but, it is, also, expected you will decline to accept it.

Thus, the argument swings back and forth, with each party proclaiming a highly virtuous position. This cycle of defiance and persistence will be seen over and over.

It looks that whenever something is offered, from a cup of tea to a piece of jewelry, an attempt is made to refuse it; and, each time an attempt has been made to refuse something, an additional insistence is shown from the other party for it be accepted. In this particular scenario, where some possession has been admired, one side occasionally wins, and the other party yields. Clearly, the more sincere party in the argument will become apparent.

Additionally, there are several tales of families selling their final possessions to feed their guests. This tremendous commitment to giving is evident across society; but, it is partly offset by the demand for modesty or humility which causes one to reject the majority of what is offered because it is more than what is deserved.

This generosity extends to even the smallest social gatherings. Whenever you consume food, drink, or smoke, you must always offer it to anyone present.

On a more general level, it is claimed that "if a person attempts to say something positive about himself, he is a liar; if there is anything positive to say about him, others will say it."

According to the Middle Eastern host and guest guidelines, the person who extends the invitation is the host. This is applicable both in the household and in chance encounters in restaurants or even informal lunch invitations.

If you meet in a restaurant or cafe, the person who is already there is considered the host and is, typically, responsible for paying the bill. If an Arab invites you to lunch, he is the host. In the Arab world, the term "Dutch Treat" is unknown. In order to safeguard your public image and standing, it is necessary to reciprocate the hospitality. Likewise, do not decline hospitality extended to you.

Hosting the Arabs

In much of the Arab world, it is essential to demonstrate hospitality in your own territory, such as your home or office. This is necessary to safeguard public image, dignity, and status. Failure to be welcoming is "one of the Arab world's sins".

When entertaining Arab visitors or guests, the host should never convey the impression that they wish to end the visit despite important business.

Americans must remember to use just their right hand while passing or eating food. The left hand is used only for personal hygiene in the Middle East and is never extended to another. If you are left-handed, you must take extra care to adhere to this practice; otherwise, you risk insulting your Arab investor.

Do not insist on an Arab removing his traditional headwear when they are visiting. Arabs consider their headcloth (ghutra) or skullcap as an integral part of their outfit, and they typically remove it only before undressing. Lastly, always accompany a departing guest outside the door or gate.

As previously stated, friendship in the Middle East is considerably more demanding compared to what it is in the West to the point that what we consider friends are considered acquaintances.

In Arab culture, a true friend is someone you feel comfortable relying on at any time, knowing that they will try their very best to support you, even if it entails a personal sacrifice. Whereas Americans develop short and casual friendships, the Arab definition of friendship revolves around endurance and intensity.

What not to do

1. Try not to take whatever you have been offered or abuse their generosity, especially If you are unsure that you can somehow return the favor.

2. In the Quran, Allah uses several Arabic words which convey the meaning of "humility." And, they have adopted this in their lifestyle. Therefore, no matter how good you are, try to be humble and do not speak too highly of yourself as it is a turn off in the Arab culture.

3. Try to be as generous when hosting Arabs as they will be when hosting you. Luxury and lavishness are rooted in their culture and cheap doesn't exist in their dictionary. Therefore, the last impression that you want to give them is that you are being cheap. You don't have to spend your life saving to host them but try to do your best.

4. Because you are in an Islamic country, you should avoid drinking alcohol or eating pork when you are with Arab business associates.

Dress Code

Most locals wear their traditional outfits in corporate environments. That entails a dishdasha for men (the long white shift) and an abaya for women (a floor-length robe).

For men, it usually consists of a long white robe known as a thobe and often incorporates a red and white checked headgear called a keffiyeh (A.K.A ghutra).

The actual style and color of this dress will differ from country to country, region to region, and even tribe to tribe. Although it is not commonly acknowledged, it is claimed that the colors of the stitching of a keffiyeh are associated with politics. One key component of wearing the keffiyeh is securing it on the head. It is seen that even when an Arab man walks swiftly, his keffiyeh never falls off, as they are using the "Igal", the black rope-like cord that keeps the keffiyeh in place.

In the GCC, most women dress in the customary black robe called an abaya and will wear a hijab.

Do not be tempted to adopt the traditional dress yourself since doing so could be offensive to individuals who wear it as a symbol of a continuous heritage and culture.

That said, ex-pats should dress in modest, non-revealing formal attire.

Men should dress appropriately in suits and dress shoes. A decent business suit will suffice (although dark and neutral colors are suggested).

However, in some regions, more casual clothes are acceptable; it's much like anywhere else in the world, depending on the country and business sector.

In general, avoid wearing shorts, short-sleeved shirts or t-shirts while traveling in the Middle East. The concept of modest attire applies equally to men and women in many societies. Remember, even Elon Musk donned a suit and tie to a conference in Dubai.

On the other hand, women should pay particular attention to their attire. Cover your chest, shoulders, upper arms, and knees at all times. Long skirts and dresses are an excellent choice because they conceal any cleavage. Alternatively, you could pair a light blazer and shirt with loose, flowing trousers. Always avoid wearing flashy jewelry and overpowering perfume.

Many Arab societies place a high value on outward appearance as a reflection of social status; high-quality clothing reflects a comfortable or powerful position within society. As a result, it is recommended that you pay close attention to the appearance and quality of the dresses you are wearing in order to make a favorable impression.

UAE Minister of Cabinet Affairs and Chairman of the World Government Summit (WGS), Mohammad Al Gergawi in a conversation with Elon Musk, CEO of Tesla, and SpaceX, during the fifth edition of WGS in 2017.

Food and Beverage Restrictions

Islam, like many religions, prescribes a set of dietary requirements for its adherents to follow. These guidelines include food and beverages that are permitted (halal) and those that are prohibited (haram) in Islamic dietary law. Some scholars believe that these laws help unite followers as members of a coherent group, while others believe that they also build a distinct Islamic identity.

Muslim believers are absolutely prohibited from eating or drinking the following foods and beverages (haram):

- Dead Meat (the carcass of an already dead animal—one that was not slaughtered by the proper method)
- Swine (Pork)
- Carnivorous Animals
- Birds of Prey
- Intoxicating Drinks
- Blood
- The meat of animals that died from electrocution, blunt force, or strangulation.
  * All seafood is halal

You might find it interesting that the term "Alcohol" is the altered version of "Al-Kuhul", an Arabic word, and today, it is wildly used worldwide.

Ironically, the ingestion of alcohol is forbidden in Islam because it is considered an intoxicant. The Holy Quran forbids intoxicants in several verses because one is not meant to harm oneself in any way or form. Therefore, most Muslims believe that the consumption of alcohol is "haram" (forbidden).

Hence, they do not eat foods that contain alcohol or drink liquor. According to Islamic scholars, the presence of alcohol in the same room does not affect the prayer, but anyone who drinks alcohol cannot pray for a month unless they repent. As the Prophet Muhammad said alcohol might have some medicinal value, there is no restriction for using alcohol for medical purposes.

Saudi Arabia and Kuwait are completely dry; there is not a drop of legal alcohol outside diplomatic compounds.
While the Gulf countries are more conservative, Bahrain and Dubai have some of the wildest bars in the region. You can consume alcohol at home and in licensed hotels, restaurants, and bars of Dubai, but once you leave the vicinity of your home or the venue, it becomes illegal to be drunk in public.
You should know that Dubai and the UAE, in general, have a zero-tolerance policy in place regarding drunk driving.

Some less conservative Muslims believe drinking is a personal decision between themselves and God; and, think moderate ingestion of some liquors like red wine can help maintain the immune system.

Egypt, Lebanon, Syria, Jordan, Morocco, and Tunisia are all quite wet; so, alcohol is available in restaurants, bars, and shops.

To summarize, I suggest taking the safe route by not serving alcoholic beverages or food to your Arab investors. On the other hand, I urge that you explore a few good "Halal" restaurants for the occasions that you have meetings with your investors in a western country.

Gifts

It is a grand gesture to give a token gift when meeting a potential partner for the first time. Similarly, giving a present upon concluding a deal is always appropriate. Gifts are, also, suitable to celebrate significant religious festivals, such as the end of Ramadan.
If you can get it from overseas, that is even better. The locals are grateful for gifts from people of diverse cultures.

Snacks such as premium dates or chocolates are an excellent choice for a first meeting. You might choose more expensive or higher-quality gifts for longer-term relationships. Additionally, a well-chosen coffee table book makes a fantastic gift.

At higher levels, you may even select pens or cufflinks from luxury brands.

It is best to avoid gift exchanges between genders. If you must deliver a gift to a lady, it is preferable to have a female member of your team present it. At the very least, you may state that it came from a female relative. The same guideline applies to a woman who has to present a gift to a male business associate.

Certain products should also be avoided as gifts, as they may offend Muslim associates. For example, refrain from giving alcohol, pigskin products, personal items, or anything associated with pork or dogs.

> Mid-December 2018: I was on my way to an Arab friend's hotel to give him a ride to the LAX airport, where I got stuck in LA's rush-hour traffic. My friend was returning to New York, where he resides; and, I wanted to meet him one more time before he left town. I also wanted to give him a New Year's gift, but it was getting late, and I was worried he might lose his flight. I eventually located a store and dashed into it to get a cologne for him, and we made it to the airport safely.
>
> The next day, he called me up and said; are you serious???
>
> It turns out that I had not only bought him a woman's perfume, but the airport agents also made him check in his carry-on as he was holding a liquid container. Fortunately, we were very close friends, and he

understood the situation and was not offended. It even became an inside joke for us later on, but that may not always be the case.

The moral of the story; I highly recommend learning from my mistake and dedicating enough time to choose a suitable gift for your Arab investors, not a gift that they are forced to share with their wives.

Islamic Calendar (Hijri)

The Islamic calendar, often known as the Hijri or Muslim calendar, is utilized for religious purposes in Arabic-speaking countries. (Nowadays, it is pretty standard for the GCC countries to use the Gregorian calendar for business purposes).

In the Hijri calendar, a lunar year is comprised of 12 full lunars (monthly) cycles, each lasting 354 days.

Except for the 12th month, Dhi al-Hijjah, the months alternate between 30 and 29 days in length. The twelfth month's duration varies throughout a 30-year cycle in order to maintain the calendar in sync with the moon's actual phases.

Thus, the Islamic calendar's New Year begins ten or eleven days earlier than the 364-day solar calendar year.

The 12 months of the Islamic year are:

1. Muharram
2. Safar
3. Rabi' al-Awwal (Rabi' 1)
4. Rabi' al-Thani (Rabi 2)
5. Jumada al-Ula (Jumada I)
6. Jumada al-Akhirah (Jumada II)
7. Rajab
8. Sha'ban
9. Ramadan (the month of fasting)
10. Shawwal
11. Dhu al-Qa'dah
12. Dhi al-Hijjah

The first day of the Islamic calendar was set as the first day of the "Hijrah", the Prophet Mohammad's migration from Makkah to Madinah on July 26, 622 C.E.

"Umar I", the second caliph, introduced the Hijrah era in the year 639 CE.

Thus, the term A.H., which stands for the Latin Anno Hegirae, or 'Year of the Hijrah,' is used to represent Islamic dates in the West.

Umar started the first year A.H. with the first day of the lunar month of Muḥarram, which corresponds to July 16, 622, in the Julian calendar.

CONVERSION

Use the following equation to roughly convert a Gregorian calendar year (A.D./C.E.) into an Islamic equivalent (A.H.).

$$AH = 33/32 \times (AD - 622)$$
Example: $33/32 \times (2022-622) = 1443$

Key Dates within the Hijri Calendar:

- Al Isra' wal Mi'raj (The night journey and ascension)
- Ramadan Begins
- Eid ul Fitr
- 1st Dhul Hijjah

- Day of Arafah
- Eid ul Adha
- Islamic New Year (1st Muharram 1444)
- Day of Ashura (10th Muharram)
- 12th Rabi Al Awwal

Women in business in the GCC countries

Women are becoming more involved in business in the Gulf Cooperation Council countries. This is due to the fact that many Arab women are getting more educated and would like to work rather than marry young.

In contrast, women accounted for 71% of university graduates in the United Arab Emirates in 2018.

Furthermore, many ex-pat women relocate to GCC countries in search of work or to establish a business overseas. Women in the workforce are supported by the government through part-time and flexible work measures, paid maternity leave, and encouraged equality in the workplace.

The United Arab Emirates (UAE) passed an equal wage law in 2018 to begin addressing the gender wage gap. Articles 27 to 24 of the UAE's Labor Code similarly protect women's rights. According to these rules, women are prohibited from working between the hours of 10 p.m. and 7 a.m. (with exceptions for technical and health services).

On the other hand, women are not permitted to work in dangerous conditions and are entitled to maternity benefits.

Attitudes toward women in business are certainly more tolerant, especially for women from the western world.

Negotiation

You may look to be an honored guest rather than an opposing negotiator.

But don't be fooled into a false sense of security by warm hospitality and civilized negotiations.

Negotiation is a welcomed diversion in the Middle East, and this is critical for anyone wanting to deal with Arab partners.

Bear in mind that Middle Easterners, in general, are always looking for the most outstanding products and services at the best possible price.

If you like to see how the world's top negotiators operate, engage in a deal with an Arab. But, when you do, keep your guard up because Arabs are born traders. This is precisely why they are so formidable at the negotiation table. Due to the fact that they have had to trade for the majority of their assets over the centuries, they have developed into the astute negotiators they are today.

Arabs are tenacious in their bargaining; so, you should be prepared to be firm but respectful.

A senior dealmaker will frequently seek concessions from you in order to demonstrate his authority; so, anticipate plenty of give and take, especially late in the negotiating process.

Providing a "buyers beware" notice may be appropriate if the prospective buyer is unfamiliar with Arab negotiation techniques. This is not meant to disparage, but rather to draw attention to the cultural distinctions between "shopping" in an Arab marketplace and shopping in a western-style center.

It is a good idea to be familiar with the concepts of how to get a reasonable value for one's money, regardless of where one shops.

Contrary outcomes may often occur due to cultural variations in purchasing and selling negotiations between Arabs and Western trading cultures. These two cultures exhibit substantial differences in their behaviors, communication styles, and social standards.

As a result, while negotiating across cultures, negotiators may bring different perspectives to the table which may result in unwarranted misunderstandings; and, occasionally, these different perspectives diminish the possibility of finding an optimal solution or reaching the desired outcomes.

If you want to do business with a specific company and see immense potential for significant business, hang tight before pitching a massive project and target the low-hanging fruit first. Suggestions for pilot programs or efforts to close smaller deals are welcome. You'll be able to focus your time and resources on more strategic high-value deals once you've established a strong relationship with the investor and persuaded him to part with more considerable finances.

The Process of Negotiation

Meetings are critical to the business culture and can take on a variety of forms. You may be required to attend formal meetings with the most senior members of the organization to discuss and negotiate or, alternatively, you might end up at more casual lunches or coffees. You may, even, be invited to dinner at someone's home in some instances.

A strong negotiator will analyze the other side's case to identify weaknesses and aim to persuade them to abandon their standpoint in favor of their own. Throughout the encounter, it is critical to constantly assess the position in light of new information from the opposing side and to monitor the opponent's reaction(s).

The initial assessment may be confirmed during the discussion; alternatively, an astute negotiator may read the signals and adapt the position to make it more appealing to the opposing side while focusing on their own objectives.

A negotiator may opt to apply pressure or make compromises during this phase in order to progress to a satisfying settlement.

Regardless of the cultural prefix, suffix, or conduct of any negotiation meeting with Middle Eastern businesspeople, the approach is essentially the same:

Stage 1: Planning; establishing objectives or specifications, compiling data, and determining a negotiation strategy.

Stage 2: Opening; this is the stage at which negotiators disclose their initial positions.

Stage 3: Bargaining; both parties have the same objectives at this stage.

Stage 4: Closing; each party will decide whether the other side is adamant about maintaining its position or is willing to compromise. Final trade-offs may result in a settlement at this stage.

* Each of these stages will be discussed in further detail in the following section.

Negotiation Tactics

PLANNING

During the planning phase, you will define the negotiation objectives.
It would be prudent to prepare for three possible outcomes:

- The least desirable scenario which only fulfills your minimum requirements
- The ideal scenario which provides the best possible arrangement from your standpoint
- And, the most likely scenario which achieves a realistic goal while providing comfort for both sides

During this phase, you should explicitly identify the bargaining parameters that could be adjusted to reach a concession. Any proposal should be designed to allow for the exchange of concessions. For instance, a consumer may accept a higher price in exchange for better payment terms.

Typically, the following factors establish the foundation for every deal or project, and they can be interpreted as bargaining parameters and trade-offs:

- **Scope, and Quality,**
- **Time,**
- **Capital (Price/Cost),**
- **Benefits, and Risks**

Scope and Quality

The term "Scope" refers to the specific deliverables. In most circumstances, there are no "acceptable ranges" for scope. We request certain products and expect to receive them in the specified volumes. The scope of work is primarily concerned with the quantity or list of deliverables.

The "Quality" factor is quite similar to the scope constraint, except that it is concerned with the attributes of a deliverable. When we discuss quality, we are not attempting to increase or decrease the quantity of a product. We are solely interested in altering or adding flexibility to ensure that a specific feature is present and meets the expectation.

Scope and quality function similarly to the other constraint factors. For example, if a project is over budget or running late, the vendor may still be able to offer the required products, but the quantity may be lowered, or some characteristics of the products may be reduced or eliminated.

Time and Capital

"Time" and "Capital" are often referred to as standard parameters; and, they are represented in our estimations which are generally presented in the form of ranges. Under the standard terminology, we are considered on-target as long as we operate within the agreed range limit.

Historically, time and capital have been the primary concerns for any party when evaluating the desirability of an offering.

This is most likely because they are the most tangible measurements and are highly interrelated.

Reduced delivery time often raises direct costs, such as labor, material, and equipment. These increased expenses will indeed affect the pricing of a product or service and its associated profit margins.

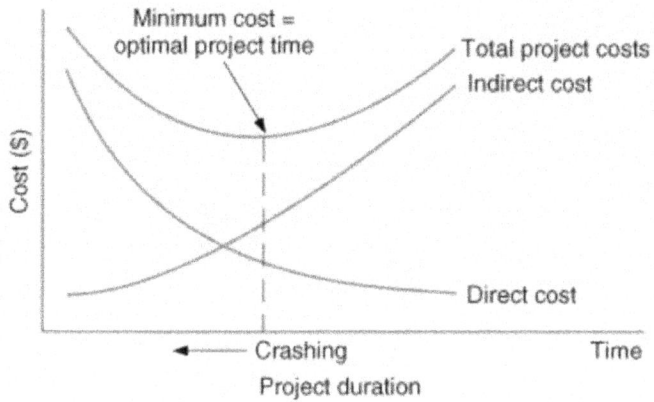

Benefits and Risk

"Benefits" and "Risk" are the model's final two elements and may be called controversial except for the fact that they are both inherent in any trade. While these two elements are not being constructed, they should be demonstrated and carefully evaluated in order to assess their interaction with the "classic" parameters (time, capital, scope, and quality).

When these two aspects are not examined and appropriately planned, they are likely to be overlooked and may have a detrimental effect on the delivery.

Benefits represent the anticipated value that the program will provide to the organization. For instance, a deal may aim to deliver a new sales system, with the value of increasing sales or improving customer service. Typically, benefits are influenced by both internal and external factors. Even if we are on schedule, within budget (capital), and fulfilling scope and quality objectives, a change in circumstances may suggest that the project is no longer beneficial.

While everyone recognizes risk as a crucial component of any deal that must be acknowledged and effectively managed through risk response strategies, we continue witnessing situations where risks were neglected and result in a disaster.

We can see that every offering will have a certain degree of risk that we are willing to take and a specific level that we are unwilling to tolerate. While risk encompasses both "opportunity" and "threats," it is managed in a similar manner.

The following triangle illustrates the relationship between these variables. When one of the variables is altered, the other variables must be adjusted to maintain the triangle's connection. If one point is shifted without modifying the other points, the project's benefits will be affected, putting the whole project at risk.

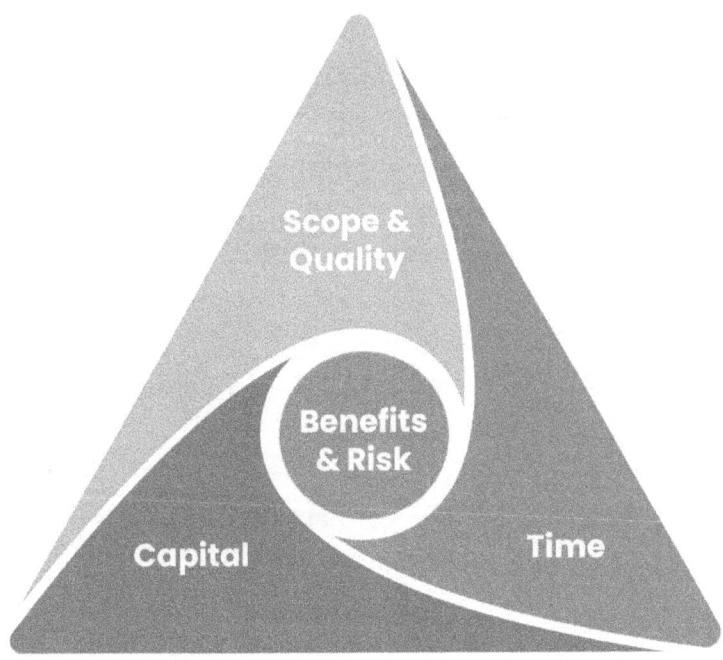

It is vital to comprehend the other party's objectives to provide a satisfactory solution that concurs with all parties.

Negotiation Team

To conduct a successful negotiation, you must assemble the necessary data and documentation well in advice in order to establish your argument and substantiate the case.

Select a negotiation team of at least two individuals; however, it would be better to assemble a group of three or more to promote your interests.

- One member should be delegated to take the lead,
- Another to take notes and provide information to the negotiator,
- And other(s) to observe the opposition and play a specific role in accordance with their briefing.

Determine the strategy and tactics; the initial offer; the actions to be taken and any compromises; as well as any arguments and supporting facts for justification.

Inform the negotiating team of their respective roles and the strategy and techniques that will be used.

All documents should be provided to the negotiating group in advance; and, you should stress the importance of presenting a consistent front at all times.

If possible, conduct a practice so the members can rehearse their assigned roles.

OPENING

The following should be the strategy for your opening:
Open with a realistic and reasonable attitude. You should thoroughly examine your opponent's requests and attitude; and, you should closely observe their behavior, especially when suggesting any resolution.

Doing so will enable you to comprehend your adversary's position and determine their strengths and weaknesses, tactics, and negotiation elements, as well as to enable you to establish a measure for determining whether they are bluffing or not.

When competing at this level, it is vital to avoid making any concessions; nonetheless, you should allow the opponent some room to maneuver while challenging his position. Maintain a non-committal attitude toward offers and explanations until subsequent phases of the negotiations.

BARGAINING

Due to the fact that bargaining is an integral part of the Middle Eastern business culture, you may anticipate substantial haggling during the course of negotiation.

In Arab culture, being able to negotiate the best possible price instills a great sense of pride and dignity in the negotiation process.

Many Western corporations, on the other hand, are misinformed about this.

Their perception is that Arabs will battle tooth and nail to obtain the lowest possible price; however, this is not the case. What they actually prize is the satisfaction that comes from knowing they have successfully negotiated the finest deal possible. When dealing with the Arabs, small gestures can make a big difference at times.

Giving Arabs a modest discount or other incentives can help them feel a sense of accomplishment. That said, companies may be able to contemplate small price hikes after taking this into consideration.

It is highly recommended to bargain "backward" whenever you are involved in a trade with an Arab. Avoid attempting to undercut him by giving a price before hearing the other party's proposal first. Assume the seller will provide you with a marked-up price for the traded service or material, and work backward, from approximately half of the suggested quote to a more moderate-reasonable price. However, do not offer a terribly low price.

Your goal here is to bridge the gap between the two opposing standpoints and persuade the other party that the case being presented is compelling.
It is appropriate to make conditional solutions, but it is not prudent to make one-sided compromises in your proposal.
Always be willing to make a concession but negotiate the entire package. The critical point here is to avoid allowing the opponent to tackle one item at a time. Your strategy should be to hold all issues open in order to maximize the benefit of potential trade-offs.
When making a purchase, consider a variety of similar products or services, including the one you would like to acquire. Then, begin pricing among these options without disclosing the product or service that has become the object of your affection. The key is to act indifferently toward any specific product or service.
Solicit quotations from sellers for three or four comparable products that you may be interested in.

You can also refer to the competitors' offerings and prices to un-stabilize your opponent's standing. Then, once you've established a clear pricing range, it is time to strike and close the deal.
You can casually say, "yeah, this one would work," referring to the object of your desire, and watch whether the opponent takes the bait. This strategy frequently succeeds, as your counterpart is typically just as desperate, if not more so. However, you may encounter resistance and end up in a strong bargaining game.

READING THE SIGNALS

It is critical to remain alert to any signals sent by the opposite party during the bargaining process. As previously indicated, body language is extremely important in the Arab world.

Frequently, a signal is communicated through the body language of Middle Eastern people. Keep an eye out for positive and negative emotions expressed through body language because these signals could be a more accurate indicator of opinion than statements.

When an opponent makes a conditional comment, he is indicating his willingness to continue the engagement. Do not be shy about asking questions because appropriate inquiries can lead to new avenues and provide new possibilities. Make a concerted effort to understand what is being said and to read between the lines.

ARGUING

Always remember to be culturally sensitive to the possibility of losing one's face because a significant portion of time will be spent debating.

The ability to think clearly will aid in presenting a proposal, sifting information, and establishing or renewing a relationship with the opponent.

It is a true skill to argue persuasively while identifying flaws in an opponent's counter-argument; and, it requires an enormous amount of practice. Nonetheless, it is important to develop this ability because it is the most significant characteristic of a negotiator.

Always be considerate of your manner / mannerisms especially when arguing; and avoid criticizing your opponent because it is in everyone's best interest to avoid a major confrontation. It will benefit your relationships and business in the long run.

Your strategy should be geared toward discrediting the argument, not the individual. Avoid browbeating your opponent; disagree, but do not insult him/her.

You must be open to listening to both the stated and implied to argue effectively. To create time for consideration, you can occasionally respond to a question received with another question; but, do not overdo this practice.

Never say "no"; instead, offer an alternative and, wherever possible, ask the opposing party to justify a proposal item by item. This will place the burden of clarification on the person who is being questioned.

Be prepared to walk away from any deal–though with caution. You should maintain a polite demeanor even if you are backing out.

At the end of the day, if you believe there is absolutely no chance for closing, it is fair to respectfully decline any further bargaining. Give them your regards, wish them well, and politely walk away.

Nonetheless, I've found that being open to walking away from a deal has occasionally been rewarding. From the Arab's standpoint, your sincere departure indicates that this deal is less important than offending each other.
By doing so, you indicate that, while it is not your fault that the deal fell apart, you still respect the other party and can part ways amicably ("ma'laish"). As a result, you may be able to pursue them later-on and persuade them to make additional concessions; and, thus, secure a better deal that is more in line with your preferences.

GAMBITS

It is vital to understand Middle Eastern culture when negotiating which is the reason why we began this book with the cultural characteristics of Middle Easterners.

Generally speaking, western executives believe that negotiating is a tool for bridging the gap between opposing viewpoints; and, they consider this activity as a puzzle that must be solved.

On the contrary, Arabs are more inclined to view the negotiation as a competition; and, as an opportunity to create and maintain honor. Arabs are far more competitive in negotiations compared to the westerners.

When negotiating in the west, compromise and concession go hand-in-hand. Westerners believe reciprocity is a necessary component of a negotiation and its absence makes a successful solution highly improbable.

Nevertheless, these assumptions are less likely to be applicable in the Middle East negotiation paradigm. Arabs realize that a solution is possible only when both parties are prepared to make concessions. Settlements can only be reached when neither party can claim complete victory over the other.

Deviating from this firmly held value will result in a significant loss of face. In Middle East culture, "Tanazul" is the act of conceding in favor of a competitor and carries strong implications of defeat and surrender.

An infinite number of gambits can be employed in any negotiation; however, they should be applied with caution and tact when negotiating in the Middle East if you want to accomplish a goal. A gambit that generates offense and loss of face can ruin your relationships and directly impact your proposal's survival.

CLOSING

A famous proverb on Wall Street says that only two emotions drive the market: "Greed" and "Fear." Despite being an oversimplification, it is valid to some extent.

When and how the agreement is achieved will be determined by the opponent's commitment to finding a deal reasonable and appealing; as a result, you should make an effort to sweeten the contract or provide your opponent with a few options during the closing phase.

Closure may occur as a result of any of the following; nevertheless, I recommend implementing these tactics in the stated order.

- You can also make a minor concession in exchange for a settlement. It is worth noting that this is the optimal time to provide a compromise rather than during the bargaining stage.

- Remind them of what has happened so far, emphasizing the compromises made and your shift from the original position. This will stress the fact that you have already made a concession and revised your position; this will appease their Greed emotion.

- Another option is to secure the contract and split the difference; or, you may even include an incentive element in the offer.

- It is risky to use threats of consequences to apply pressure on your counterparty because it can be highly destructive in the context of saving face. However, it is still an option that you can employ with prudence in order to elicit the Fear emotion. You may argue that the deal's failure would result in unfavorable publicity for both firms. In this manner, you avoid singling out your opponent and reduce the likelihood of losing face.

Take your time, and don't be pushed into making a decision. Make a final offer only if you are willing to carry it through and deliver on it. The credibility of your offer will be eroded if it is not genuinely final, and the opponent calls your bluff. Additional concessions will be required to rescue the deal in that instance, so proceed cautiously with your approach.

Maintain a positive tone and avoid committing to the word "final" and devaluing it; instead, state that this is the furthest you are prepared to go.

Lastly, I must mention that tea is typically served at the completion of a negotiation venture; thus, drinking it earlier would likely interfere with an "actual" agreement. Despite the fact that tea is merely tea, it represents a ritual in the Arab world that brings people together. Moreover, it serves as a sweet ending to a delightful negotiation.

Negotiation Summary

Negotiating with Arabs can be complicated and challenging because, while they may be solely focused on pricing in some situations, they typically consider a number of factors. Therefore, offering additional incentives to bridge the gaps and secure a settlement may be prudent.

Nevertheless, the convention is that regardless of what transpires during the negotiation, both parties strive to come to an agreement.

Although off-the-record discussions are widespread, they should not be referenced during the formal bargaining phase unless your opponent consents in advance.

Make sure you understand the distinction between a firm and a conditional offer because a firm offer will be used to construct the final agreement and cannot be withdrawn.

If your business plan is solid, you've done your homework, and you're prepared to embrace a unique social and business culture, 2022 is shaping up to be a great year to plunge into the ambitious, rapidly expanding economic zone that is the GCC. However, you should know that Arabs often make decisions on gut and heart feelings, not necessarily on facts, figures, and projections; this is why you need to consider the other factors that were covered previously.

How to Pitch to Arab Investors

If you're just getting started and have never raised capital before, your chances of raising a billion dollars are slim. It is recommended to begin with singles and doubles, build momentum and, then, step up your game to raise more significant sums. You should practice hard, master your game, and develop confidence before playing in the big boys' club.

Similarly, if you're looking to seek funds for a start-up or first-time fund, you're unlikely to approach Arab investors. Sovereign wealth funds do not get out of bed for deals worth less than $100 million; therefore, utilizing investor networks, such as InwestCo, that have established relationships with Arab investors will benefit you greatly.

Being represented by InwestCo will give you a reputable presence and recognition that would, otherwise, have taken many years to build.

It's essential to match up with who you're targeting size-wise; then, narrow it down further to access the actual intent of the investor(s) you are targeting.

You need to penetrate the market and properly position yourself by identifying potential investors in advance so you can target your audience appropriately and make your presentation materials truly meaningful for your targeted investors.

You want to figure out, specifically, the actual investor types you're going after so you can dial everything into what they value most.

In the next sections, you will be walked through the requirements needed to be applied when pitching to Arab investors.

Drafting your pitch deck

In order to target your potential investor appropriately, you need to have a clear understanding of who you are, your focused market, your competitors' offerings and strategies, and your product (service) differentiation.

Now, the question is how do you determine whether your firm is properly positioned?

Oprah Winfrey once said: "Challenges are gifts that force us to search for a new center of gravity. Don't fight them; just find a new way to stand."

Interestingly, this quote is the fundamental concept of Marketing Research and translates as follows:

(What is needed in the market) – (What is available in the market) = New Opportunity(ies)

By following this methodology, you can easily investigate the market, determine what is currently available and what is yet missing, and uncover market gaps. Thereby, you may confidently position your company and target your niche effectively.

Economist Joseph Schumpeter stated that entrepreneurs create value "by exploiting a new invention or, more generally, an untried technological possibility for producing a new commodity or producing an old one in a new way, by opening up a new source of supply of materials or a new outlet for products, by reorganizing an industry or similar means".

Entrepreneurial innovation, according to Schumpeter, is the disruptive force that generates and sustains economic progress; but it has the potential to destroy established businesses, change industries, and disrupt employment in the process. He coined the term "creative destruction" to describe this phenomenon.

Schumpeter defined business procedures, including the concept of downsizing, as those that aim to boost an organization's efficiency.

Businesses' dynamics develop the economy and improve our standard of living. However, certain developments, such as those brought by technology, can have unintended consequences.

Schumpeter believed that this cyclical destruction and reconstruction is essential in a capitalist economy and that the entrepreneurs are the primary driver of economic growth. He argued that the ultimate goal is progress, and that progress begins with the introduction of fresh ideas and approaches.

Later on, Schumpeter introduces the following factors for identifying a new business opportunity:

- Create a new market for an existing solution.
- Find new resources that will allow the entrepreneur to create the goods cheaper.
- Repurpose existing technologies or integrate solutions to produce an old product in a new way.
- Create a new product using existing technologies or integrating solutions.
- Finally, develop a new product using new technology.

Your venture should include at least one of these elements, if not more. Ideally, you may introduce a new or improved product or service to an underserved market via a more effective distribution route.

Once you have a clear understanding of your offering, your niche, and product differentiation, you need to develop a way to describe your position in a simple sentence.

You must construct a simple one-liner that precisely describes what you do; emphasizes your strength and credibility; declares your background and further; and, reveals the characteristics that differentiate you from your competition.

Investors, typically, do not invest in things they do not understand; and the more valuable the potential investor, typically, the busier they are; so, it may be harder to get their attention. This is why you need every advantage possible to; meet with, attract, add value to, and convey all to clients or investors.

WWW.INWESTCO.COM

Branding

When you meet for the first time, it takes only a glance, perhaps three seconds, for someone to evaluate you. The first impression is formed by the quality of your information and materials, your appearance, your body language, your demeanor and mannerisms, and the way in which you dress. You are examined with each new encounter.

These initial impressions are nearly impossible to reverse or undo, and they frequently set the tone for the subsequent relationship; this is why you must strive to make an excellent first impression.

As a general rule, no one will ever take you more seriously than the way you carry and portray yourself.

If you have a pitch deck handout that appears to have been developed in a high school class or a $50 logo purchased from an outsourcer for one hour of labor; you will ultimately appear cheap or inexperienced; this something you should avoid at all times, especially when working with Arab investors.

1976   1977-1998

On the left, you can see Apple's initial logo (created in 1976), and on the right, you can see their second design (established in 1977). Apple's branding strategy is emotion-driven, and its identity is characterized by its emphasis on lifestyle, imagination, creativity, innovation, passion, technological strength, and most importantly, simplicity.

Their superior product quality, sophisticated branding strategies, and user-friendly features provide them an advantage. This distinct positioning enables Apple to charge a premium for its products while maintaining market share and dominance.

I'm confident that Steve Jobs and his team recognized the critical significance of branding and representation from the early stages where they opted to change their logo after only a year.

By examining the images on the previous page, you can see how their logo evolved over the course of a year, becoming simpler, dynamic, yet more eye-catching.

It should go, without saying, that you have to quit emailing investors from Gmail or Yahoo and invest some money to obtain a domain, professional email address, etc.

Over the course of the last 16 years, I've worked with many fresh entrepreneurs who were just getting started on raising capital for their ventures. Interestingly, some of these entrepreneurs seemed unwilling to invest even a tiny sum of money in themselves to refine their business plans or simply to fine-tune their pitch deck material; yet, they expected others to throw millions into their venture.

Bear in mind that the first step toward earning Arab investors' trust is to present yourself as an established, hands-on professional; and, as a result, making a poor presentation (either in terms of content or cosmetic) is the worst damage you can do to yourself and your reputation.

A lousy logo or brand name is repulsive to some investors; and, can hurt your ability to get in the gate or secure funding.
Your brand name should be straightforward, catchy, and informative so that Arab investors and future customers easily understand what you're doing without having to conduct research. You may use your own name as a brand only if you

are a well-known individual, confident that your name would add legitimacy to your firm and create synergy; otherwise, using your name is not encouraged.

Your brand should be unique, appealing, and valuable; this ensures that your audience understands what you're doing and wishes to collaborate with you. When people see your logo, brand, and one-liner altogether, they should be sucked in, lean forward, and feel it was crafted only for them. They think, "I've never seen anything like that before" or "I was unaware such a thing exists".

There is a serious problem if the business does not have a teaser. Worst-case scenario: they're on page six of your pitch deck and still have no idea what your firm does or why they should care that you exist. The one-liner and brand alone should be enough to convince them to schedule a meeting with you. You can, also, use your one-liner on every voicemail, email, Ad, and most importantly, on the first page of your pitch deck.

The name and logo should be tailored to your industry's unique characteristics, challenges, strengths, investor base, and competitors. Additionally, when creating a logo, consider utilizing colors that appear good on both white and black backgrounds.

It is worth noting a targeted approach (sniper shot) to a desirable audience type will be more appealing than a generic approach (shotgun aim). Often, we see organizations with higher intentions remaining generic out of fear of missing out on investors or consumers they do not have yet.

Narrowing your audience may require you to exclude 5%–15% of the population that does not fit your niche; but, if you lack momentum, you will need to apply multiple fresh ideas to get things in order.

Concentrating your aim can assist you in growing your revenue through increased turnover when vending with customers; and, it raises the likelihood of your being funded when seeking investors; hence, focusing on a target that commonly works will assist you in acquiring greater traction.

Content Localization

In this section, I will dive into the importance of implementing proper localization when drafting your pitch deck, website, or any material that you will be presenting to your investor, so your presentation meets the expectations and norms of the Arab culture.

In order to apply a successful localization, you have to take the cultural and technical dimensions that distinguish the Middle East region and the Arabic language into account. Although the possibility of localizing your material may seem daunting, it's essential to engaging Middle Eastern investors and is certainly worthwhile.

When adapting your content to the Middle East region, you should acknowledge and navigate the differences between your own culture and your target culture.

Customizing your Pitch Deck for the Middle East region may involve revising symbols, humor, images, videos, colors, and customer representations.

When adding pictures and videos to your content, make sure your characters are dressed in a way that reflects Middle Eastern standards and meets with Middle Easterner's conventions regarding appropriateness and formality. If your brand uses animals in its marketing material, you may wish to revise that choice; you may also want to reconsider the music used in your brand videos.

Apart from these "fundamental" considerations, you'll want to identify and incorporate trends that make your content more relatable, engaging, and relevant to their sociocultural backgrounds.

A case in point for cultural sensitivity is advertising funeral services; Arabs find this repulsive. Arabs have a great deal of regard for their elders; so, they find this type of content to be upsetting and disrespectful. Although, purchasing a funeral plan for a living parent is considered a nice gesture in several western societies.

Needless to say, your content should avoid sexual appeal or erotic innuendoes. The content of your pitch deck should be conservative, and the appearance should be devoid of any social attitudes or situations that are incompatible with Arabian culture or Islam. Your message should emphasize the quality and functionality of your product or service.

Arabs maintain a conservative demeanor in public. Additionally, it's worth emphasizing that in Arab culture, spouses' feelings are kept private. While younger generations are less rigid, they retain strong beliefs in their social and cultural norms; and, as a result, it is advisable to hedge your bets and avoid exhibiting affection in your marketing content; make it non-existent.

Additionally, you should be aware that laughter and joking are toned down in public; this is not the case in private meetings.

Here, you may compare the Coca-Cola advertisement broadcast in Saudi Arabia to their commercial televised in the United States. It is an excellent practice to list the distinctions.

While it is unnecessary to translate your content into Arabic as most GCC investors are fluent in English, it would be an excellent gesture to include a few lines in their language.

You can solicit the help of InwestCo's business advisors when producing such materials or ask a local translation/advertising agency to deliver the job. Nonetheless, we strongly advise against using Google Translate or any other automated solution, as the algorithms in these services are not advanced enough to digest the context; hence, the final result may be disastrous.

If you choose to work with a local translation service provider, ensure that they have a thorough understanding of the language, your business, your audience, and the market you wish to penetrate.

Making a word-by-word translation of your current product literature will not necessarily prove to be a practical equivalent of the original; and, in some cases, might yield the opposite of your intended message. Each market operates under its own set of marketing and advertising guidelines, and each audience is approached differently.

I am sure that you have heard about some companies' dilemmas in changing the name of their products when introduced to a foreign market because an exact translation proved to be ineffective or, in some cases, offensive.

Business Cards

Every employee of the company should be provided with a business card. Your business card should include the following information: your firm's name, your first and last names, your title, phone number, email address, and website URL.

Aside from that, the card should be available in both Arabic and English.

When exchanging business cards, make sure to hold the other person's card in both hands and carefully study it before putting it away.

When handing somebody a business card, always use your right hand; doing it with your left is considered disrespectful.

Additionally, ensure that the card's Arabic side is facing upright.

One Liner

A one-liner is a single sentence that simply describes what your firm offers and why customers should do business with you. It assists you in organizing the framework of your one-pager, pitch deck, or website, among other things; and, should underpin all communications with your audience. It's essential to your becoming crystal clear about what you offer and how it benefits your customers.

The issue that the majority of business owners encounter is that they are too close to their operation and industry to simplify and express their message effectively. However, once you become crystal clear (as opposed to believing you are becoming crystal clear), things begin to shift dramatically in your business, and this transition may be rather thrilling.

A perfect one-liner should express the issue your customers are facing, your strategy for overcoming it, and the method your product or service will utilize to improve their lives. It should accentuate your product differentiation, distinct value-added approaches, and strong positioning as the group that adds the most value.

To summarize, it should state:

- What you do?
- Where you do it?
- When you do it?
- How you do it?

- What component of your business is most appealing to investors, or what makes you distinctive or compelling?

This is not difficult or expensive to implement; you don't really need $1 million in revenue or $100 million in assets to accomplish this. If investors want to know what you do in a single captivating statement that costs nothing but your time, why would you not prepare one?

We've learned that your initial presentation should be tangible, captivating, original, and verifiable. You should say something no one else is saying or can say.

Examples:

Amazon's One Liner:

"We want to be earth's most customer centric company; to build a place where people can come to find and discover anything they might want to buy online."

InwestCo's One Liner:

InwestCo is an exclusive investor club that pairs entrepreneurs with the right investors in order to make long-lasting relationships.

Best Pitching Practices

There is a firm intention for positioning this chapter before the pitch deck development section because these instructions are vital for strategizing your presentation. It is needless to say that a good presentation strategy will lead to developing a successful pitch deck that engages the audience and maximizes your exposure.

Remember that nothing kills a presentation faster than reading from a slide deck. Reading the presentation slides creates two impressions in the minds of Arab investors; you either lack preparation or you lack confidence; and, it is not a good look either way.

Additionally, reading from a slide deck conveys the message that you do not appreciate your audience's time because, if you did, you would have put more effort into your presentation.

It's not the products, data, or companies that people connect with; it's the stories.

As an entrepreneur, your job is to weave the information into a story that people can relate to. This makes people more likely to hear what you have to say and sense the need for your offering. Having a powerful story enables you to confidently address your audience and educate them on the solution that will transform their lives.

Slides should not be the primary means of conveying information; instead, they should highlight the points being made.

If the primary attention is on the words you speak, then anything that appears on the screen should only serve to support and enhance them. While tabling bullet points and analyzing what each one entails may be tempting, you should avoid listing your bullets on the screen. The remarks on the screen should serve as the background to your presentation.

People are much more likely to recall images than words, and when they do, they will recollect what you were discussing; thus, you should choose your photos intelligently in an effort to maximize synergy.

Of course, there are times when using words makes sense, but my general rule is that no slide should contain more than 20 words unless you're sharing a quote.

Another reason you should avoid reading your slides is that you will be losing eye contact with your audience. If they do not connect with you, they will certainly not connect with your story.

Try to engage your audience; perhaps by asking questions or having the audience members vote on the information you've presented, a personal connection and relationship can be established. You want to think of what the prospect may be wondering, worried about, or challenging in their head and not saying.

Standing on stage and facing the slides creates a barrier between you and your audience as you're both focused on a display instead of each other. It is acceptable to look up to check where you are; but, relying, solely, on your slides to recall what to say conveys your insufficient preparation.

In fact, you should have practiced your narration so many times that it flows out effortlessly. Once you're in front of the audience or on the platform, your brain will be rushing with a million thoughts; therefore, you must rehearse your speech numerous times until it becomes muscle memory.

If you concentrate on a single type of investor, you can customize 80% of what you say and do, as well as where you do it. Additionally, you can learn about their common headaches, train of thought, worries, fears, and obstacles and address them upfront. A best practice is to openly address the elephant in the room and either remove it or object to it. It's as if you're designing a maze; and, as they travel down the corridors toward your solution, you close the windows. Instead of creating an escape route, you guide them to the logical conclusion of moving forward.

Finally, you must maintain credibility while using humor, visuals, graphs, colorful language, and other elements that disrupt typical assumptions about what will happen next. This move teases the information consumer, makes the information more memorable, and lowers the likelihood of the audience going on in boredom or indifference.

By the way, have I mentioned that InwestCo offers Pitch Deck review and revision services? Our extensive experience working with private equity firms, angel investors, venture capitalists, and private investors enables us to provide an array of client services that are strategically designed with our investors' appetites and mandates in mind. Our design experts can assist you in creating your **Logo, Marketing Material**, and **Visuals**, while our experienced business advisors will help you develop your **Business Case, Executive Summary**, **One-Pager**, **Pitch Deck**, and **Website** using our successful strategies and your vision.

Pitch Deck

There are many ways to make a pitch deck, but the most common is PowerPoint, Prezi, or Keynote.
You will often use your pitch deck during a web-based or face-to-face meeting with investors, clients, partners, and co-founders.

A good pitch deck should be focused primarily on the areas where investors are most curious to learn about your company.

If you're presenting to an audience that is already familiar with your sector, you should avoid spending an excessive amount of time describing the fundamentals. For instance, if you operate in the self-storage or rental housing industry, avoid dedicating 12 slides detailing how apartment building function and collect rent.

The more complicated, perplexing, and elite the industry, the more attention must be paid to it. For instance, if you are involved in blockchain, oil and gas royalties, biotech/pharma partnerships requiring FDA approval, or complex hedge fund strategies, it is best to focus more on making your approach and your investment area very clear and easy to understand.

Quality of Your Material

The cosmetics and the quality of the presentation and the package are as crucial as the quality of the content, especially when dealing with high-caliber investors. Make sure you are using thick, rich paper (preferably glossy paper) and that your content has been printed using maximum quality.

There is no need to remind you that you are dealing with Arab investors, and your handout should feel outstanding and luxurious, so they don't mind carrying it with them.

The color scheme for presentation slides is a vital decision that must be made early in the development process.

You should inspect the colors, mainly if you're using a colored background, ensuring you're utilizing the proper colors that are easy to read and won't wear out your readers over time.

The best colors for slides are those with high contrast, making them immediately visible. I recommend utilizing light text and bright accent colors on dark backgrounds and dark text and bold accent colors on light frames.

Applying these measures enables your audience to read the text easily while interacting with the presentation's forms, graphs, or shapes.

Given these general interpretations, you should avoid employing too many colors; and, I recommend avoiding excessive use of black, orange, gray, red, and brown as they might be perceived as overly passive or aggressive.

Numerous studies have demonstrated that different colors elicit various emotions in many people. Considering this fact is critical when choosing colors for your presentation slides because you want to avoid colors that detract from the content you're giving.

Here are some interpretations for different colors.

Color	Emotions that are elicited
Black	Heavy, mournful, highly technical, formal, death
Blue	Peace, tranquility, trust, confidence, security
Green	Nature, environment, health, reptiles, insects
Gray	Conservative, practical, reliability, security, staid
Orange	Warmth, expansive, flamboyant
White	Purity, reverence, cleanliness, simplicity, heaven
Purple	Royalty, wisdom, spirituality, mystery
Red	Passion, excitement, love, intensity, heat, aggression
Yellow	Optimism, happiness, idealism, imagination
Brown	Earth, simplicity, outdoors

There are a few specific colors that should never be combined for a number of reasons; here are some examples:

- **Red and Blue** - these two hues lack the contrast necessary to be appropriately seen when combined. This combination appears to lose even more contrast when projected on a screen.

- **Orange and Blue** - another combo that has an unsettling effect on readers because the colors appear to vibrate in opposition to one another.

- **Red and Green** - these two colors clash and make reading extremely difficult. Additionally, folks who are colorblind will have difficulty deciphering what you are attempting to convey in the presentation.

The Cover

An outstanding cover page establishes the tone. Consider the cover slide to be a movie trailer, providing an overview of the narrative. It enables the investor to comprehend the information that is about to be revealed.

Your pitch deck's cover should ideally be glossy when printed, and the information should be published to the highest possible quality. The cover page should have your logo, title, website URL, and, most importantly, a one-liner.

We've seen numerous pitch decks that include a disclaimer and a confidentiality notice, a table of contents, and an overview of the business. Yet investors have no idea what you're delivering halfway through (at which point they've already lost some of their enthusiasm) because the brand offered no hint; therefore, I highly recommend placing your one-liner on your cover sheet.

Pitch Deck Content

Dense, unpleasant text is widespread, as are lengthy presentation decks. Your pitch deck should be between 12 and 19 pages in length and no longer than 25 pages. Arab investors, in general, are extremely busy and lack the time or patience for lengthy pitches.

Consequently, you must keep in mind that they do not have two hours to peruse your pitch deck. Even your own team, partner, or spouse are unlikely to read a 40- or 60-page document precisely.

I will not be going into the technical details of your pitch deck component as there are numerous books on the subject, and I am assuming that you are well-versed in creating business plan material. However, our team of InwestCo business consultants can assist you in developing business cases, financial projections and analyses, executive summaries, and websites, among our other offerings. Please feel free to contact us for any professional consultation; our team of professionals will gladly assist you.

Having said that, you may incorporate the following topics into your pitch; but, you are not required to cover all of them, and some may be left in the Appendix section or tabled for later conversations.

- Industry Analysis
- The Target Market Description
- The Need and the Business Opportunity
- Your Product/Service Differentiation and your Unique Value Chain

- The Competition Analysis
- Strategic Position and Business Model
- Projections, Metrics and Financials
- Roadmap and Timelines
- Organization structure, CAP table and Management Team
- Contact Information

When working with ultra-wealthy Arab investors, they may seek to negotiate custom terms or conditions and request that they be incorporated into your presentation or the following paperwork. Additionally, you may wish to include your assumptions, privacy statement, and disclaimer at the start of your pitch deck.

Your team slide's principal objective is to instill confidence in your team and your ability to make the enterprise a tremendous success. It is customary to provide a brief biography for your key team members, including education, relevant experience, and notable accomplishments. Profile photographs eliminate anonymity and humanize what may otherwise be cold exchanges. Your audience benefits from visual confirmation that they are working with a real person.

Your team members' photographs should be professional, well-done, and clean to appear as someone you would do business with. You want it to seem professional and approachable to facilitate business growth. It sounds simple, but so many people have an arm around them that was cut off in a wedding photograph, a hazy or grainy photograph, and a variety of different backgrounds for their team.

Professional visuals are essential to enhancing the quality of your pitch and attracting potential investors to consider your enterprise seriously. Most significantly, they may convey your message in a fraction of the time and space required by numerous pages of text.

The average person responds far better to visual information than just plain text; therefore, diagramming and visualizing your opportunity, it's unique value chain, or process is vital to having a great pitch deck.

> As an example, I was reviewing a pitch deck to construct a luxury Caribbean Resort & Residences in Bay Island. My client already owned the land and was interested in finding a partner to build the resort. The client noted there are abundant partnership opportunities for complementary services such as zip-lining and jet-skiing because of the location's proximity privileges, but, the pitch deck had several rendered pictures of the rooms.
>
> However, these pictures were not what I expected to see as an investor, even though they were designed and eye-catching.
>
> First of all, I didn't know where the Caribbean Bay Island was before googling it; and, secondly, I didn't know where the resort would be located on the island to assess the proximity to the other potential complimentary businesses. Thus, it would have been more beneficial to provide a map indicating the island's position, the resort's

placement on the map, and the possible locations of potential partners. You should avoid including images solely for the purpose of having them in your publication.

Utilizing visuals in presentation is an effective instrument when communicating with someone unfamiliar with your company or your specific opportunity; and, even though, all pitch decks should include rich, instructive graphics and diagrams, fewer than ten percent of pitches do so in practice.

As an illustration, the Unique Value Chains of Amazon and InwestCo are depicted in the following section, demonstrating how helpful a visual may be for the audience to better comprehend your narrative.

Amazon's value chain

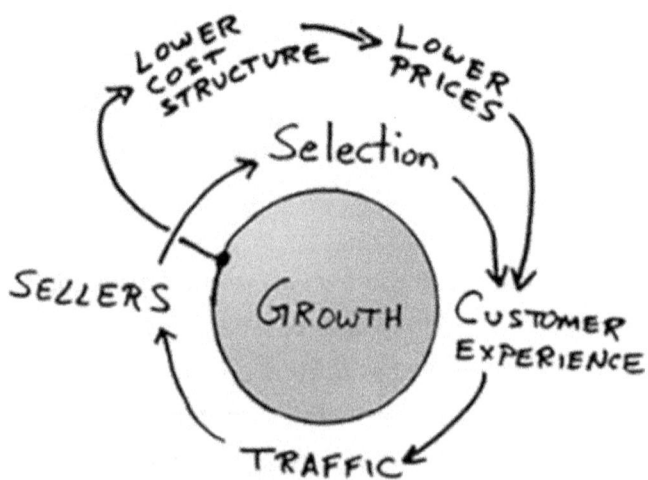

InwestCo's Value chain

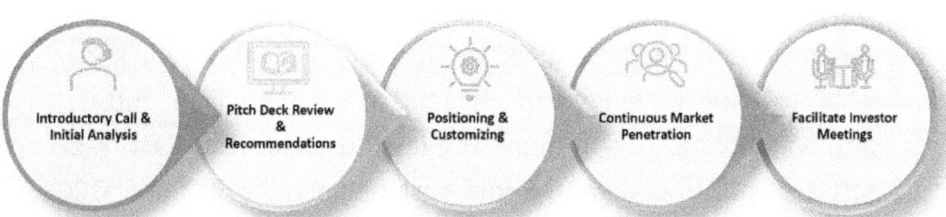

Introductory Call & Initial Analysis	Pitch Deck Review & Recommendations	Positioning & Customizing	Continuous Market Penetration	Facilitate Investor Meetings
• First call screening • Goal planning • Setting timelines • Establish a roadmap	• Review your material • Feedback & insights • Suggested Revisions • Optional Edits	• Targeted exposure • Customized marketing • Tailored geographical approach • Vast investor reach	• Explore your niche • Continuous Market Penetration • Thought leadership • Educational content development	• Investor screening • Detailed Planning • Exceptional execution • Successful investor meetings

Conclusion

The Middle East outlook and potential business opportunities are very promising and attractive. But, just when you think you know what to expect, things can change; or progress in a, mostly, positive direction; but, none-the-less, change. The fast-track series of reforms in the Middle East is meant to position GCC countries to better compete for technology, tourism, and investment.

This has never been more evident than last month, when Wynn Resorts, a major American casino developer, announced a multibillion-dollar deal with Ras al Khaimah, a UAE emirate, for a massive luxury resort, doubling down on its bets on the Middle East market where gambling was historically prohibited.

Resort plans include:

- a 1,000-room hotel
- 10 restaurants
- Multiple lounges
- a spa
- a convention facility
- shopping venues
- and, most importantly, a gaming area

Yes, a gaming area; but, the question is whether gambling is synonymous with gaming in this instance.

We may get a hint from the Ras al-Khaimah Tourism Development Authority's establishment of a new bureau, the Department of Entertainment and Gaming Regulations, to regulate integrated resorts such as the one planned by Wynn.

However, because this project is still in the early planning phase and will not be completed until 2026, no one, not even the developer (Marjan), is verifying details at this moment.

Due to its glamor and glitz, the UAE is frequently compared to Las Vegas, except Islam prohibits gambling.

Surely, circumstances are shifting to offer the UAE an edge over its Middle Eastern neighbors. This wave of change has long authorized the consumption of alcohol and the wearing of bikinis on the beach (making the UAE a favored ex-pat center).

Wynn Resorts' new CEO, Craig Billings, has described Al Marjan Island, home of the new resort, as "a pristine setting and ideal greenfield location." Al Marjan is a man-made island less than an hour away from Dubai International Airport, making it the perfect tourist attraction/location.

All seems to be in order for a successful project; and the new Gaming Regulator will ensure responsible gaming while protecting the "social, cultural, and environmental landscape of the Emirate and covering the licensing, taxation, operational procedures, and consumer safeguards."

Regardless of the outcome, this project illustrates the immense economic potential they perceive, justifying the risk they are taking; and, I am convinced that they have done their studies and are not the only western firm with a favorable view of the Middle East market.

As you've learned herein, the ways that Middle Eastern Investors evaluate their future partners may be a bit different than what you may have expected; but, at the end of the day, all investors want to minimize risk while getting big returns on their investments. Therefore, make sure you are presenting the key ingredients they are looking for before approaching any investor, Middle Eastern or otherwise. That's why having InwestCo on your team can make all the difference.

The bottom line is Middle Eastern investors will be upfront about asking you exactly what they are getting into, i.e., "what the business has accomplished and what still needs to be accomplished". And in order to show sincerity and respect, you should demonstrate your integrity by revealing any possible interference from external factors such as:

- Which regulatory or legal issues may come up?
- Will your product or service need significant adjustments to be suitable for ten years from today?
- Have you budgeted enough money to cover everything?
- Do you foresee an exit from the investment?
- Will there be a chance to see a return at various stages of the investment?

There's no way to guarantee you'll be successful in obtaining the money you are looking for; but it's guaranteed you'll have a much better chance of doing so when you prove commitment. This can be done by putting your money where your mouth is; yes, openly show potential Middle Eastern investors how much of your own cash, time, and other assets are already in your venture.

You'll be doing this during the getting to know you / socializing / dating period; not during your formal pitch; just another reason why having experienced guidance on your side is so… important.

When you start dating a Middle Eastern investor, interest is high, and trust is low. So, no matter how short, the dating period is all about increasing trust for a successful partnership. Time spent engaging with a Middle Eastern investor is never wasted. Typically, a pleasant meeting is the most valuable step to obtaining your desired Term Sheet.

And, when you clinch the deal, should you be worried about the legal work associated with the closing and strategies you should follow; no, if you have the proper guidance. This is just another reason why you need InwestCo.

It's also the topic of my upcoming book, **"The Three Comma Club Strategies,"** where I'll disclose the Five Top-Secret Business Strategies I learned from Middle Eastern Billionaires.

www.ingramcontent.com/pod-product-compliance
Lightning Source LLC
Chambersburg PA
CBHW050911160426
43194CB00011B/2366